Defence and diplomacy

NEW FRONTIERS IN HISTORY

series editors

Mark Greengrass
Department of History, Sheffield University

John Stevenson
Worcester College, Oxford

This important new series reflects the substantial expansion that has occurred in the scope of history syllabuses. As new subject areas have emerged and syllabuses have come to focus more upon methods of historical enquiry and knowledge of source materials, a growing need has arisen for correspondingly broad-ranging textbooks.

New Frontiers in History provides up-to-date overviews of key topics in British, European and World History, together with accompanying source material and appendices. Authors will be focusing upon subjects where revisionist work is being undertaken, providing a fresh viewpoint which will be welcomed by students and sixth formers. The series also explores established topics which have attracted much conflicting analysis and require a synthesis of the state of the debate.

Forthcoming titles

Jeremy Black
British politics in the eighteenth century, 1714–93

David Brooks
The age of upheaval: Edwardian politics, 1899–1914

Conan Fischer
The rise of the Nazis

Mark Greengrass
Points of resistance in sixteenth-century Europe

Tony Kusher
The holocaust and its aftermath

Alan O'Day
Irish home rule

Panikos Panayi
Immigrants, minorities and British society, 1840–1919

Daniel Szechi
The Jacobite cause

Michael Braddick
The nerves of state: taxation and the financing of the English state, 1558–1714

Ciaran Brady
The unplanned conquest: social changes and political conflict in sixteenth-century Ireland

Defence and diplomacy
Britain and the great powers
1815–1914

C. J. Bartlett

Manchester University Press
Manchester and New York
Distributed exclusively in the USA and Canada by St. Martins Press

Copyright © C. J. Bartlett 1993

Published by Manchester University Press
Oxford Road, Manchester M13 9PL, UK
and Room 400, 175 Fifth Avenue, New York, NY 10010, USA

Distributed exclusively in the USA and Canada by St. Martin's Press, Inc., 175 Fifth Avenue, New York, NY 10010, USA

British Library Cataloguing-in-Publication Data
A catalogue record for this book is available from the British Library

Library of Congress Cataloging-in-Publication Data

Bartlett, C. J. (Christopher John), 1931–
    Defence and diplomacy: Britain and the Great Powers, 1815–1914/
C.J. Bartlett.
        p.   cm. — (New frontiers in history)
    Includes bibliographical references and index.
    ISBN 0–7190–3519–8. — ISBN 0–7190–3520–1 (pbk.)
    1. Great Britain—Foreign relations—19th century. 2. Great
Britain—Foreign relations—1901–1936. 3. World politics—19th
century. 4. World politics—1900–1918. 5. Great powers.
    I. Title. II. Series.
    DA530.B364   1993
    327.41—dc20   92–38136

ISBN 0 7190 3519 8 *hardback*
ISBN 0 7190 3520 1 *paperback*

Typeset in Hong Kong by Graphicraft Typesetters Ltd.

Printed in Great Britain by Bell & Bain Limited, Glasgow

Contents

Contents

Introduction

The purpose of this volume is to analyse how the British – by a combination of defence and diplomacy – contrived between 1815 and 1914 to protect their home territory, empire and world-wide network of communications and interests from their leading enemies. At first their quarrel was primarily with France, Russia and the United States. Towards the end of the period Germany began to take the place of the Americans. But Britain's subsequent *ententes* with France and Russia, together with her declaration of war on Germany in 1914, did not mean that Germany had become the only danger. The *entente* with Russia in particular was also designed to limit that empire's competition with Britain. From 1911 similar considerations were at work in the renewed Anglo-Japanese alliance.

Not surprisingly, this period of extraordinary influence and activity on the part of the British has and continues to be the focus of much scholarly research. Many important studies have appeared relating to this period since Kenneth Bourne produced his major synthesis, *The Foreign Policy of Victorian England*, in 1970. At that time he noted the need for more work on Aberdeen, Palmerston, Clarendon and Grey among British ministers. British foreign policy between 1905 and 1914 was among the areas in need of study, while the army had been greatly neglected.

Some – but not all – of these gaps have been or are being filled. If some controversies have lost their former vigour, others have arisen in their place. Among the many that might be listed, the following are of particular relevance in the present study. In what circumstances, if any, was it possible for the British to be indifferent

1

to the state of the balance of power in Europe? How successful were they in their simultaneous pursuit of interests in Europe, Asia, America and Africa, and what sort of priorities did they establish between these continents? What external as well as domestic reasons enabled Britain to preserve her position as the world's largest naval power? To what extent were the fundamentals of British defence policy challenged in these years? Was the empire simultaneously a source of strength and weakness? Did Britain exaggerate the dangers from France, Russia and the United States? When and to what extent did the Anglo-German antagonism really begin to eclipse Britain's rivalries with the other powers? How far did Anglo-German differences contribute directly to the outbreak of war in 1914? And does the period from 1815 as a whole serve as a reminder of the need to be on one's guard against extravagant claims concerning Britain's power and influence even at her peak as a great and imperial state?

Muriel Chamberlain adopts an admirably sceptical approach in her *'Pax Britannica'?: British foreign policy 1789–1914* (1988). The question mark in her title is crucial. Was there a Pax Britannica, and if so how should it be interpreted? As long ago as 1964, G. S. Graham entitled a chapter 'The illusion of "Pax Britannica" ' in his study, *The Politics of Naval Supremacy*. He noted that, when 'Pax Britannica' was first used by Joseph Chamberlain in 1893, its originator was thinking of the benefits which British rule had brought to India. W. N. Medlicott commented in 1968 (*British Foreign Policy since Versailles*, p. 326) that the peculiar quality of Britain's world authority 'had lain in the fact that it was dominant only where it encountered no serious great-power competition'.

It is evident, for instance, that Palmerston's 'gunboat diplomacy' was a usable instrument against only weaker states or peoples. The navy might also be employed to 'show the flag' in dealings with the great powers – a British diplomat at the Algeciras conference in 1906 drew comfort and strength from the presence of major British warships in nearby Gibraltar. But these were only tangible expressions of the total power which the British had to be able to mobilise in a real emergency.

It is true that the French Revolutionary and Napoleonic Wars had clearly underlined the influence that Britain could exert through her financial and economic resources as well as with her navy and (sometimes) her army. Particularly impressive had been her capacity to wage a long war and continue to subsidise the opponents of France. Her statesmen were able to draw upon the high reputation earned during the war era (1793–1815) for at least another forty years. A Frenchman commented in 1821:

> Thus, from one centre, by the vigour of its institutions, and the advanced state of its civil and military arts, an island which, in the Oceanic Archipelago, would scarcely be ranked in the third class, makes the effects of its industry and the weight of its power to be felt in every extremity of the four divisions of the globe . . .[1]

Similar descriptions abounded through the nineteenth century, inspired by British national pride or foreign amazement, fear and jealousy. Thus Britain was variously described as the 'workshop' and the 'financial capital' of the world, the 'mistress' (or the 'tyrant') of the seas, and the 'empire on which the sun never set'. There was even talk of a 'Pax Britannica'. The British were widely (then and later) credited with great manipulative powers even in Europe. A German scholar, Michael Stürmer, wrote recently (*Guardian Weekly*, 9 August 1992) of the balancing role which Britain 'exercised so masterfully' in Europe in the nineteenth century.

Nevertheless, over the period as a whole between 1815 and 1914, there was a relative decline in Britain's security as other powers industrialised and increased their wealth. The development and spread of railways began to erode some of the advantages of sea power around the coasts of Europe, Asia and North America. The competition offered by France and Russia (especially the latter) tested British influence in many parts of the world. The United States and Japan began to emerge as considerable players within their own regions. Finally, the unification of Germany led to the emergence of a European power with the ability and ultimately the inclination (however confused) to bid for hegemony in Europe itself. As time passed the British found it more and more difficult to provide answers to these varied challenges to their international position and pretensions.

Given the fact that Britain was simultaneously a European, America, Asiatic and an African power, her foreign and defence policymakers (despite the great resources at their disposal) faced more complicated problems than any of their rivals. There was hardly a corner of the world where she might not find herself in dispute with the local people and – much more seriously – with a rival

3

great power. This made it all the more important that British diplomats should succeed in limiting the number of enemies ranged against their country at any one time. But the diplomats in their turn required the material backing of the armed forces. As Frederick the Great once observed, diplomacy without arms was like music without an orchestra. Even with the world's largest navy, however, successful statecraft was heavily dependent on the openings provided by the weaknesses, distractions and divisions of Britain's opponents. The British took pride in their ability to 'muddle through', yet the wisest among them were equally conscious of their debts to others and their own good fortune.

The position was well summed up by a Foreign Office official (Eyre Crowe) in 1907: 'It would therefore be but natural that the power of a State supreme at sea should inspire universal jealousy and fear, and be ever exposed to the danger of being overwhelmed by a combination of the world.'[2] Despite such fears, the British still tended to treat alliances as instruments of last resort. Yet this only made it all the more important for their diplomats to manoeuvre as dexterously in peace as in war, and so place their country in the best possible position in relation to all the powers in anticipation of any emergency.

Not surprisingly the nation's leaders at their most confident could be moved to pursue policies of restraint and conciliation for reasons of defensive self-interest as well as very different ones in the pursuit of national aggrandisement. Thus Palmerston, for all his belligerent reputation, appreciated that tact as well as firmness and shows of strength might help to protect the national interest. It was also apparent to all but the most innocent and idealistic that Britain benefited from the existence of a moderate degree of friction among her major rivals. On the whole, however, her leaders were less persistent and skilful in the incitement of such tensions than was claimed by their enemies abroad. More often it was a matter of advantage being taken of the opportunities created by others. These were frequent enough for alert and perceptive diplomats to find the means to manage or even defuse crises, and if necessary cultivate the support of temporary allies. Meanwhile when other powers, singly or in conjunction, failed to maintain a consistent challenge, the value of Britain's defence forces was accordingly enhanced. Unfortunately these favourable openings could also encourage complacency and inertia, with damaging results in the longer term.

British interest in the European balance of power was the theme of many speeches and appeared frequently in statements on foreign policy. But the balance in fact meant different things to policy-makers during the whole period under review. It might indeed mean support for the weaker against the stronger side – the classic interpretation. Alternatively, a stronger power could be tolerated if it upheld the status quo. Similarly, a desirable balance might mean one which increased British freedom of manoeuvre elsewhere in the world, or simply one which released Britain from active involvement in Europe. Neither the balance itself, nor any British response, was a straightforward matter of mathematical calculation. The highly personal views of key ministers and the prejudices of important sectors of public opinion could further complicate the equation.

International policy could not be treated in isolation from domestic politics. Foreign, colonial and defence ministers might often lament the disparity between British interests and the means provided for their protection, but other cabinet ministers – save in times of obvious crisis – were more susceptible to the expectations of their party supporters and to the electoral and economic implications of costly foreign and defence policies. Institutional conservatism and vested interests also, at least until the 1900s, discouraged radical change in the organisation and thinking of the army. This was also true – if to a lesser extent – of the navy. Despite the many crises and periods of alarm, systematic appraisal of grand strategy and defence needs were rare occurrences at best before the twentieth century. A major theme of S. R. Williamson's book, *The Politics of Grand Strategy, 1904–14* (1969), is that the famous expeditionary force which was sent to France in 1914 was 'a polit-ical expedient which bore little correspondence to actual British needs or obligations'.

Key decisions were usually taken by ministers on an *ad hoc* basis, assisted by some broad assumptions based on past experience. In the end, the degree of co-ordination between and the respective influence of interested departments was largely determined by the personalities of and relations between individual ministers. Crises might bring flurries of activity, but even the Crimean War had less enduring effects than at one time seemed possible. Again and again the British relaxed after a crisis had passed, or they persuaded themselves that they could live with the consequences of, for instance, the rise of the United States or the transformation of Europe between 1859 and 1871. Even in the case of Germany in the subsequent century, the response was selective and much governed by economic and domestic political considerations.

Britain, in any case, could not expect to retain indefinitely her original advantages as 'the workshop of the world'. Her ongoing possession of the world's greatest naval and mercantile fleets was not axiomatic. These could be surpassed by a rival or rivals blessed with the necessary resources and sense of purpose. British feelings of vulnerability increased particularly from the mid-1880s, mainly at first in the context of a possible combination of France and Russia. This had serious implications for British influence in the Mediterranean and Near East, and the security of many interests from the north-west frontier of India to the Yangtse River in China. In these circumstances, parts of the empire could seem almost as much a liability as an asset.

It is true that by the end of the nineteenth century the British were able to bring about a substantial improvement in their re- lations with the United States, but this was soon more than offset by the rise of Germany. It was not long before they had to contem- plate the possibility of sending an expeditionary force to assist France against Germany, and this in its turn encouraged demands (however unrealistic) for compulsory military service. Even at sea there were problems. Quite apart from the new German navy, it was secretly acknowledged in the Admiralty that the Americans, if they chose, could become the world's greatest sea power. Thus, the British had very pressing reasons to try to remove causes of friction with their transatlantic 'cousins'.

Balfour as Prime Minister advised the King in 1903, 'The interest of this country is now *and always* – peace.' Salisbury had observed in 1871: 'The organisation of our military system imposes upon us a *rôle d'éffacement* . . . Consequently a power of deliberation is all that is left open to us in European affairs.'[3] Even in the case of Palmerston, much caution and calculation had often lain behind the public show of pugnacity and confidence. In practice it had been Castlereagh, Aberdeen and Gladstone who had gone furthest in the search for a peaceful and stable international order, a search that had extended to the United States as well as to the European great powers. Nor had they been wholly unsuccessful, even if in practice they had often bought no more than a breathing space. Yet for

6

much of the century, frequent changes in the international environment had not seriously challenged the assumption that 'the
dimensions of policy were largely unchanging' – whatever the variations in tactics and temperament of those who controlled British
policy.[4] In contrast from the later 1880s, a rivalry of a more consistent and comprehensive character was becoming the norm. The
interludes of relative quiet were less frequent. British ministers
found that diplomacy itself required increased backing from the
armed forces, just as the latter needed extra help from the diplomats to keep their own tasks within bounds.

Notes

1 C. Dupin, *The Commercial Power of Great Britain*, London, 1825, vol.
1, pp. v–vi.
2 Paul M. Kennedy, *The Rise and Fall of British Naval Mastery*, New
York, 1976, p. 158.
3 K. Wilson (ed.), *British Foreign Secretaries and Foreign Policy from
the Crimean War to the First World War*, London, 1985, p. 17.
4 P. Hayes in T. R. Gourvish and A. O'Day (eds.), *Later Victorian
Britain, 1867–1900*, London, 1988, p. 173.

1

Consolidation and adjustments
1815–38

Castlereagh and the quest for stability

The change in Britain's position and prospects between 1812 and
1815 was remarkable. One false dawn had succeeded another in
the wars with France since 1793, and in 1812 Britain had even man-
aged to blunder into an additional and unwanted conflict with the
United States. There were problems, too, when the continental
powers began to seize the initiative from Napoleon after his disas-
trous Russian campaign. Their successes at first seemed to promise
advantages for them rather than for Britain. It seemed possible, late
in 1813, that Russia, Austria and Prussia might settle for a compromise peace with Napoleon – a peace whose detailed terms would
take insufficient account of British interests. The persistent contribution of sea power to the weakening of France and the sustenance
of the allies was not always fully appreciated or acknowledged
in Europe. The main British effort on land was far away in Spain
and south-western France. Nor had the massive subsidies to allies
over the years been automatically rewarded with commensurate
influence.

At the end of 1813 the cabinet was sufficiently disturbed to send
Lord Castlereagh, the Foreign Secretary, to the Continent to deal
in person with the allied leaders. Yet the dramatic improvement
in Britain's bargaining position which soon followed was not simply the result of Castlereagh's personal influence with Metternich
(the Austrian Chancellor) and Alexander I (Tsar of Russia). He
was assisted both by Napoleon's diplomatic errors and by his

temporary military successes in the first months of 1814. On the one hand Napoleon failed to take advantage of the possibility of a compromise peace with Britain's allies: on the other, his skilful military manoeuvring and counter-offensives shook the confidence of the leaders of Russia, Austria and Prussia. They became more appreciative of British military and financial aid and hence more sensitive to British opinions and interests. Metternich also found in Castlereagh a useful ally against the more ambitious aims of Russia.

The Foreign Minister was thus soon reporting to London: 'The fact is that . . . our engagement [at sea, on land and in subsidies] is equal to theirs united. . . . What an extraordinary display of power! This, I trust, will put an end to any doubts as to the claim we have to an opinion on Continental affairs.'[1] The French historian, Thiers, in his *Histoire du Consulat et de l'Empire*, written in mid-century, was particularly impressed by Britain's financial contribution. A modern scholar (J. M. Sherwig) made the happy choice of *Guineas and Gunpowder* for the title of a study of Britain's contribution to the defeat of Napoleon.

Such were the circumstances which helped Castlereagh to emerge as a leading European statesman. Napoleon continued to assist his rise. Exiled after his overthrow in 1814, the Emperor briefly regained power in France in 1815. At the hard-fought battle of Waterloo the British played the leading part. The victory made the British commander, Wellington, a European hero, and greatly enhanced his country's diplomatic influence in the final negotiations.

Overall, in the lengthy search for a peace settlement in 1814–15 the British enjoyed considerable success – especially when tested against the objectives which Castlereagh and his colleagues had initially set themselves. These included the enhancement of Britain's own island security. Despite Trafalgar, the French naval presence at Antwerp had continued to cause concern. This had to be ended. As one minister remarked, 'Antwerp and Flushing out of the hands of France' were worth 'twenty Martiniques' or West Indian sugar islands in British possession. Castlereagh contended that to leave the arsenal of Antwerp in French hands meant the virtual imposition of a 'perpetual war establishment' on his country.[2]

At sea, one of the great weapons used by the British had been that of war against enemy trade. The British were determined to uphold their claims to interfere with neutral shipping in the search for enemy goods and contraband of war. Despite the resentment which this had caused, Castlereagh was able to insist that British claims in this regard were non-negotiable. They were essential if sea power was to be used to full effect as an instrument against an enemy's economy. Finally the defeat of France and the war-weariness of the rest of Europe meant that Britain emerged in 1815 with the greatest measure of naval supremacy in her history.

The wartime conquest of a number of key strategic points around the world was similarly confirmed at the peace settlement. These bases were useful both in themselves and through their denial to a rival. They included Malta, Mauritius, the Cape of Good Hope and Heligoland. Malta facilitated British operations in the central and eastern Mediterranean; Mauritius and the Cape added to the security of the route to India. On the other hand, some colonial conquests were returned and used as bargaining counters so that the maritime power of France would be 'restricted within due bounds by the effectual establishment of Holland, the [Iberian] Peninsula, and Italy in security and independence'. In other words, some colonies were traded to strengthen the barriers against future French expansion. Others were restored to try to conciliate France herself (see Document 1).

Britain also needed to exclude enemies from as much as possible of the European coastline which bordered her own shipping lanes. Equally she wished to be able – as in the past – to deploy naval power as appropriate from her own bases and from ports in the Baltic, the Iberian peninsula, Italy and elsewhere in the Mediterranean. From such bases she would be able to support and supply allies as well as carry out military and naval operations on her own. The navy, for instance, had been able in the recent wars to harass the French as they tried to maintain their line of communications along the Corniche road between Nice and Genoa (described by Jomini, a French student of war, as a 'horrible route . . . under British cannon-fire').

Just as sea power had secured the island homeland from invasion, so it had usually been able to preserve British trading contacts (however tenuously) with parts of Europe even when the nation's economic and military difficulties had been at their worst. Many important Baltic ports had been kept open for much of the war – their closure between 1810 and 1812 highlighting the importance of the raw materials and British goods exchanged with that region.[3] A British admiral in the Baltic at that time needed the skills of a diplomat as much as those of a first-class seaman.

In the course of the war as a whole, trade with Europe and the wider world did more than help Britain to finance her own war effort, and to subsidise that of others. Through the control of goods from outside Europe, she was able to add to the strains within Napoleon's empire and network of alliances, thereby adding to the incentives to defect on the part of those states which were tiring of French hegemony. All this was in addition to the direct economic pressure being exerted by the navy on France herself.

Nevertheless, the recent wars had confirmed yet again that Britain could take the offensive on the Continent only with major European allies. Even Wellington's successes in the Peninsular campaign had been dependent on Portuguese and Spanish support, and on Napoleon's distractions elsewhere. Castlereagh therefore sought strong allies in the heart of Europe itself as well as security around the periphery. This explains his interest in the fusion of the Dutch and Austrian Netherlands, the establishment of Prussia on the Rhine, the strengthening of Piedmont in north-western Italy, and the entrenchment of Austria in Lombardy and Venetia as a second and stronger line of defence.

Indeed, he was interested in more than security against France. The better the overall balance between the powers, the better the prospects of peace among them. This too might be expected to favour British interests, both strategic and economic. Finally, the better the equilibrium, the greater the ease with which Britain might hope to throw her weight one way or the other in war or peace. Castlereagh went still further. He looked for ways to encourage the internal stability of the states of Europe. Admittedly his part in the redrawing of the map of Europe and some of the new internal political arrangements became the subject of much criticism at home. But the objectors took too little account of the realities of power in Europe in the context of 1814–15 and the limited options which were open to the Foreign Secretary. Protest was all very well, but both the will and means to implement their recommendations were lacking. Britain, too, desperately needed a period of peace during which to recoup her finances and to find outlets for her exports. The government also wanted peace in the hope that the revolutionary fires might finally burn themselves out, and that there would be no cause to fear, as Castlereagh undoubtedly did during Napoleon's Hundred Days in 1815, the lurking presence of 'much Jacobinism' ready and waiting to take advantage of any allied defeat.[4]

The Foreign Secretary's approach to the internal political problems of European states was strikingly – even ruthlessly – pragmatic. Thus, the character of the regime in any particular country was less important than the extent to which it promised to bring internal and external peace and stability. To that end he was ready either to accept autocracy, or to encourage modest political reform in the light of the current political condition of the state in question. He supported the restoration of the Bourbons to France in the hope that through the institution of a limited constitutional monarchy they might bring France back to peaceful habits both at home and abroad. It did not make sense to deepen the French sense of grievance or to put the restored Bourbon monarchy in the position where foreign adventures might seem the best way to win support and popularity at home.

Nor did he forget that France herself might be needed to help uphold the balance of power (she had already been involved on the side of Britain and Austria in a dispute with Prussia and Russia over Saxony in the winter of 1814–15). Russia continued to cause some unease, given the unpredictable temperament of the Tsar, the recent achievements of its army, and the projected size of its peacetime military establishment. Efforts to conciliate France were extended at the Congress of Aix-la-Chapelle in 1818. The British in any case had reason to show themselves models of restraint. The war had added considerably to their power and influence in the world, and such success excited jealousy abroad. The French protested that Britain was the tyrant of the seas, and accused her ministers of manipulating the balance on land to her advantage.

Outside Europe Britain was becoming particularly interested in India. By 1815 any maritime dangers from a major power to the sub-continent had been eliminated, although possible overland threats continued to receive some attention. Russian expansionist activities in Asia were carefully studied, though Professor Yapp[5] suggests that much of what was written by contemporary officials and agents in India and by other interested parties was really designed to persuade ministers in London to approve more ambitious policies in India. The main threat to British rule and trade came from the native peoples themselves. Thus the Russian spectre was often invoked to justify further British advances and conquests in India's north-west regions. Nevertheless, the possibility could not be discounted that anti-British feeling among the Indians might be encouraged merely by the impression that Russia was becoming a potent neighbour. Russian relations with Persia and the Muslim states of Central Asia were natural matters of concern for the Raj in India – and sometimes for ministers in London as well.

By and large, however, policy-makers at home in the years following 1815 were more troubled by Russian activities in Europe and the Mediterranean than by any in Asia. Soon after 1815 the Tsar or his agents seemed suspiciously eager to cultivate influence in Spain, or to act in 1818 against the North African Barbary states by way of a maritime league. Both could be interpreted as steps to secure naval and political advantages at Britain's expense, notably in the Mediterranean. Russia was now joining France as the European power with which the British were most likely to find themselves in serious competition. Muscovy had made great advances territorially since the 1790s at the expense of Sweden, Poland, the Ottoman Empire and some Asiatic peoples, and it was credited with the ambition and resources which could lead to serious upsets to the status quo in Europe and the Near East of even greater consequence than in Central Asia.

Meanwhile the War of 1812 with the United States had demonstrated to the British the difficulty of campaigning effectively against this transatlantic republic at tolerable cost to themselves. In the end Lord Liverpool and his colleagues had been happy to settle for a draw. The belligerents were able to end the fighting by the Peace of Ghent in December 1814 – but only by agreeing to differ over many of the issues which had caused the conflict in the first place (notably the question of Britain's claims to the right of search over neutrals at sea). At least the British had had the satisfaction of frustrating attempts to conquer parts of their own territories in North America.

At the same time the Americans were still seen as a disconcertingly energetic, self-confident and ambitious people whose acquisitiveness was expected to increase in line with their numbers, resources and vanity. In addition, many British conservatives feared that the more republicanism and democracy prospered in the United States, the greater would be their appeal elsewhere. In other words, the United States was seen not only as a conventional competitor, intent upon territorial, mercantile and even naval expansion, but as an alternative political model to Britain's more modest experiment in representative government. Here was another version of the revolutionary threats which Castlereagh feared in Europe.

But whatever his fears concerning the United States, Castlereagh was determined to see what patience and conciliation could achieve. On many issues he was reconciled to the belief that only time itself might supply answers. As he remarked to two American delegates: 'Let us, in short, strive so to regulate our intercourse in all respects as that each nation may be able to do its utmost towards making the other rich and happy.' He was encouraged to take this line since even during the war many New Englanders had insisted on continuing to trade with Britain. Lord Liverpool in 1820 publicly stressed the growing importance of Anglo-American trade. 'Every man, therefore, who wishes prosperity to England, must wish prosperity to America.'

It is true that this did not prevent ongoing trade and shipping rivalry in some parts of the world. There were, for instance, important disputes affecting the West Indies until 1830. In addition, London kept a close watch on American territorial ambitions. But here the British were at a disadvantage in that, unlike the Americans, their attention had to be directed towards Europe, parts of Africa and still more of Asia, as well as the New World. They could not lightly enter into a dispute in the Americas. Not surprisingly Castlereagh advised that Yankee 'insolence' should be met with 'great delicacy'.[6]

Thus British ministers took a far from complacent view of the future despite the many ways in which their country's international position had recently been improved. Their search for the appropriate foreign policy was not helped in the first post-war years by an upsurge of British insularity and by an understandable preoccupation with distress at home, the price of corn, the burden of taxation and other domestic problems. As for those who did retain an interest in foreign affairs, many condemned all signs of British association with the reactionary powers of Europe and their so-called 'Holy Alliance'. To such views Castlereagh paid as little attention as his political position at home permitted. He argued that it was essential to try to perpetuate the wartime alliance, and to ensure that Britain was not friendless in the event of its collapse.

While it survived he used his personal relationship with the temperamental Tsar to try to limit Russian activity.[7] British diplomatic involvement was also necessary if Metternich and the Austrians were to retain some respect for and interest in the British tie.

Thus Castlereagh made one of the most determined and distinctive efforts by any British Foreign Secretary to follow the path of co-operation (as well as that of conciliation) with the other powers. At times, indeed, he used the language of principle as well as of expediency to impress the merits of his thinking upon cabinet colleagues and European leaders alike. His rhetoric even included hints of ideas which were to be articulated much more comprehensively in later years by Gladstone and Woodrow Wilson. In 1818 he wrote enthusiastically of 'a new discovery in the European Government', and he more than once made plain his desire to escape from 'the cobwebs' and trickery of the 'old diplomacy' (see Document 2).

But if there was enthusiasm, there was also calculation. He urged his European partners to put aside the dishonesty and fierce competitiveness of the 'old diplomacy' of the eighteenth century, and to work consistently for peace and ordered change. Britain's current strength and 'insular position' allowed her to take the lead in this experimental pursuit of 'a more generous and confiding policy'. As we have seen, Castlereagh had good self-interested reasons to proceed on these lines.

Although his high hopes of the 'new diplomacy' were not fulfilled, these policies at least limped along until his suicide in August 1822. In his last years Castlereagh – with mixed but not wholly unsuccessful results from his point of view – was still making use of his personal credit with continental statesmen to try to prevent or control international action against unrest in Spain, Spanish America, Germany and Italy. In company with Metternich he worked on Alexander's dread of revolution to discourage precipitate and unilateral Russian intervention in support of the Greek uprising against the Turks. Just before his death in 1822 he was developing ideas for limited diplomatic co-operation by the powers to allow for evolutionary political change in both Greece and Spanish America, as well as to avert foreign intervention against the revolutionaries in Spain. His prospects were uncertain, but they were not necessarily hopeless. Castlereagh's policies, however, died with him. His successor, Canning, lacked both his personal contacts in Europe and his inclination to cultivate Metternich, the Tsar and other leading figures.

Castlereagh himself was probably less influential than he has sometimes been portrayed. He was much assisted by the exhaustion of the powers after the great wars. Their fear of revolution also discouraged moves to revise the territorial status quo. Even the competition that existed could help Castlereagh. Thus Metternich welcomed British diplomatic support in some of his dealings with the Tsar. All this provided ample scope for intelligent statecraft, but the time would come when diplomacy would require more substantial backing. Britain ceased to be a continental land power when the army of occupation was withdrawn from France in 1818. Even naval supremacy did not automatically invest her with power, though it might usefully signal national interest and intent.

Post-war defence policies

At the end of the war, amid all the hectic activity associated with the demobilisation of the army and navy, a brief attempt was made by those in authority to take a long view of Britain's defence needs. First and foremost the question of naval supremacy was not in dispute – it was only a matter of what margin of superiority should be sought in the light of the international situation and the state of the economy and opinion at home. But basically the strength of Britain's leading naval rivals provided a rough-and-ready guide. It was more difficult to find a comparable yardstick for the army over and above the minimum number of soldiers which were clearly required for home and colonial defence and internal order. There was a fleeting hint in the autumn of 1815 that ministers might have had something more ambitious in mind. Palmerston as the Secretary at War informed the House of Commons that the full extent of savings in expenditure on the army could not be known until the post-war establishments of the other powers had become known. But it was not long before the national dislike of a large standing army, and still more the formidable pressures for economy, put paid to any such notion.[8]

The government's financial difficulties were intensifed in 1816 when Parliament refused to tolerate the continuance of Pitt's wartime tax on income. Castlereagh warned the Prince Regent that

16

– after servicing the national debt – the revenue would cover only
£12 million out of a total government expenditure of £30 million
– two-thirds of which was spent on the army and navy. The government for the time being would have to borrow to cover the
excess, but major economies could not long be delayed. Wellington
himself reluctantly agreed that distressed finances were more likely
to weaken Britain than further disarmament. A parliamentary select
committee in 1818 argued that financial and economic strength
merited at least equal attention alongside navies and armies.

But this comment – while sensible and unexceptional in itself –
offered little practical guidance. The defence estimates were frequently challenged despite some government attempts to gauge the
mood in Parliament in advance of its submissions.[19] Critics made
much of the fact that Britain was spending more on the armed
forces than she was in the interludes of peace during the eighteenth century. But this was in large part a result of the continuing expansion of Britain's overseas commitments. The army was
now usually the more expensive service. Furthermore, over time,
this rise in costs was more than offset by the growth of the economy. Once the post-war economic crisis began to ease, the nation
was better able to afford these larger peacetime establishments
than in the years before 1793. Defence expenditure averaged only
some 2 or 3 per cent of the Gross National Product between 1815
and 1865. This compared favourably with the eighteenth century.

As colonies proliferated, so too did the garrisons. But control of
the seas was becoming even more important. Population growth
was making the nation increasingly dependent on imported foods.
Foreign trade provided a livelihood for a large proportion of the
industrial workforce. Cotton imports alone increased fourfold between 1810 and 1850, and two-thirds of the cotton goods pro-
duction was exported by the 1860s. The same was true of some 40
per cent of the nation's iron and steel products. The tonnage of the
British mercantile marine more than doubled between 1827 and
1860, while faster passages meant that the volume of cargo was still
larger. All this was reflected in a fairly consistent expansion of the
fleet from the early 1820s. The number of seamen and marines
roughly doubled between 1822 and 1852. A reforming First Lord of
the Admiralty did manage to achieve major financial savings in the
early 1830s, but thereafter down to 1852 the estimates and personnel rose broadly in step – each by about 50 per cent.

The Admiralty in December 1815 set out in detail its own estimate of Britain's naval needs (see Document 3). But its targets of around 100 ships-of-the-line and 160 frigates ready for or actually in service proved far too ambitious. Nor were they strictly necessary. In 1830 the figure was reduced to around eighty capital ships. The effective battlefleet, however, numbered only fifty-eight in 1835–8, or perhaps ten fewer than the total number of Russian, French and American sail-of-the-line afloat.[10] The French navy naturally continued to attract attention, but the naval aspirations and activities of Russia – and sometimes those of the United States – were closely monitored. The need for a two-power naval standard was never really in question. Indeed, provision against a triple threat was sometimes recommended. In the late 1820s the Admiralty took account of American as well as French improvements in ship and gun design. Furthermore, the expansion undertaken in the late 1830s meant that by 1841 the British battlefleet afloat (some seventy-three ships in all, albeit with only forty-two of the largest class) just outnumbered the combined strengths of France, Russia and the United States. The First Lord of the Admiralty, in a memorandum of September 1841 drawn up for the guidance of his successor, insisted that continuing superiority over all three rivals was essential. The three-power standard was again mentioned as a possible requirement in 1858.[11]

At the same time ministers were alive to the value of diplomacy in trying to reduce the risk of simultaneous clashes with all three or even with two of these rivals. One of the basic rules of thumb in British foreign policy at this time was the prevention of a Franco-Russian alignment. Care was also taken to try to minimise American opportunities to exploit British embarrassments with other powers. As it happened, these rivals sometimes took decisions of their own which settled the matter in favour of the British. But it was not until the weakening of Russian naval power as a result of the Crimean War, the neglect of the American navy after the Civil War, and the preoccupation of the French with the growing military threat from Bismarck's Prussia that one minister could confidently remark (in December 1870): 'we are more than equal to meet any force which in any probable (I had almost said possible) circumstances might be brought against us.'[12] Serious worries about foreign competition at sea did not revive until the 1880s.

The army, though usually receiving more funds than the navy

between 1815 and 1895, was still in effect the poor relation. The navy was almost always assured of more public support and favour. Richard Cobden qualified his own assaults on power politics and arms extravagance by insisting that in a crisis he would support whatever funds were required to maintain British naval supremacy. Nor was it difficult to assess the needs of the fleet in the light of the apparent threats posed by its obvious rivals. The implications of defeat at sea were readily understood – for the British Isles themselves, for trade and for the empire.

The army's extensive commitments did not save it from considerable reductions after Waterloo.[13] Its wartime strength in excess of 200,000 was more than halved. Wellington, who sometimes relieved his frustrations with exaggerated forecasts of disaster, grumbled on one occasion that there were not enough soldiers to form a proper guard of honour for the funeral of a field marshal. Increasing imperial commitments, reinforced by the invasion panics of the 1840s, in due course pushed the army's strength back above the 100,000 mark. There were, in addition, the troops of the East India Company, so that on paper the numbers looked impressive even by the standards of some European powers.

Nevertheless Britain's regiments were always widely scattered, and there were no reserves of consequence to act in Europe. The prompt dispatch in 1826 of 4,000 troops to support the Portuguese monarchy was no more than a signal to other powers, and was sufficient to meet the local situation in Lisbon. As the Crimean War was to reveal, even with increased numbers from the 1840s, the army continued to prepare itself essentially for internal security, duty in various garrisons and fortresses, and imperial soldiering. The army at home suffered from a debilitating round of recruiting, basic training and assisting in the maintenance of domestic law and order.

Some ministers, as they struggled to reconcile competing calls for security and economy, looked for relief by a reduction in the numbers of troops committed to the colonies. Lord Grey as Secretary of State for War and Colonies in the late 1840s attempted to devise a 'coherent philosophy of imperial defence'. He believed a larger reserve at home made good strategic and political sense. He hoped that troops in the white colonies would be replaced in part by local militias. These could be reinforced from home as necessary by the new and 'easy communication' made possible by the development of steamships. Steam would similarly amplify the protection supplied by the Royal Navy. Over the next twenty years some progress was made on these lines – but this was often driven by the search for economy rather than inspired by sound strategic calculation.[14]

Admittedly an impressive network of bases was in process of creation – despite the difficulties in providing properly for their defence. As early as 1816 Castlereagh told the Commons, with only a little and pardonable exaggeration, that Britain 'had acquired what in former days would have been thought romance – the keys of every military position' to secure the empire against military attack. Singapore was added in 1819 and Aden in 1839. Control of Hong Kong was confirmed in 1842, and there were other miscellaneous gains. Gaps did exist in the northern and eastern Pacific. Storeships positioned in Valparaiso in 1843, and Callao in 1847 were a poor substitute, so that the Admiralty cast ever more covetous eyes towards Vancouver Island and (briefly) San Francisco Bay.

The advent of steam added to the fleet's requirements. Bases had now to keep stocks of coal and help with engine repairs. The inefficiency of the early engines and problems of coal supply (as well as service prejudice and tradition) encouraged the continued use of sail as much as possible. But interest in steam grew rapidly in the middle of the century as ships fitted with auxiliary engines and screw propellors demonstrated their capabilities. The Admiralty in January 1852 suspended work upon all sail-of-the-line under construction in the expectation that all capital ships would be steam-assisted in the near future.[15]

The navy was helped, too, by the fact that – however irregularly – some squadron and fleet exercises took place. The development of steamships and improved guns provided some stimulant to the study of naval warfare, even if in practice the technical problems associated with the new equipment absorbed most attention. The navy, whatever its limitations, remained a force 'in being' to an extent unknown to the army. Squadrons or fleets could be assembled and dispatched across the globe. The instrument – however blunt or rusty – could be sharpened, while in the Board of Admiralty itself there existed an institution and the personnel which, though heavily burdened with routine administration, could at a pinch provide rough-and-ready strategic direction.

In contrast, no fewer than eleven authorities competed rather than co-operated to manage the army. The complexity of the administration baffled most contemporaries. This, coupled with the weight of tradition, vested interests and the character of most of the army's duties, meant that it became, as the Prince Consort later remarked, not much more than an 'aggregate of battalions'. There was little in the way of manoeuvres to pull it together temporarily or to provide a serious intellectual challenge. The establishment of a training camp at Chobham shortly before the outbreak of the Crimean War highlighted the deficiencies. 'This Army is a shambles,' commented one disillusioned artillery officer.

Attempts at reform were repeatedly defeated or severely curtailed by vested interests. Further untidy compromises resulted. Deep-rooted civilian distrust of a standing army, and equally deep-rooted military distrust of the civilians impeded constructive dialogue. The main responsibilities continued to be shared out between the Commander-in-Chief, the Secretary at War, the Secretary of State for War and Colonies, and the Master General of the Ordnance (whose department also provided guns for the navy), while the Commissariat was under the control of the Treasury between 1816 and 1854. Any attempt at a brief summary of the responsibilities of each would almost certainly be misleading.[16] The confusion and competition left the Prime Minister and key ministerial colleagues to act as a final (and usually much delayed) court of appeal. Not surprisingly, continuity and systematic study were at the mercy of politics, personalities and current circumstances.

An attempt was made in the late 1830s to extend to the army the centralisation of naval administration which had been achieved by Sir James Graham at the Admiralty in 1834. The creation of a 'Minister of War' to oversee the whole was mooted. But Wellington, until his death in 1852, was one of the most formidable obstacles to change. In some areas he was a true diehard, especially in questions of administration. He defended the Board of Ordnance despite its separation from the army and its lethargy and other defects. He opposed the suggestion that there should be a chief of staff, arguing that these duties could be done perfectly well by the Commander-in-Chief. Here he was misled by his own success from Assaye to Waterloo. In particular he thwarted the proposals of a Royal Commission in 1837 for one cabinet minister to have overall responsibility for the army, and through whom the cabinet would pass its instructions to the Commander-in-Chief. Wellington feared such proposals would leave the army yet more exposed to the whims of ministers and Parliament. He suspected, with reason, that many politicians were more interested in economy than military effectiveness (see Document 5).

Meanwhile, in the first forty years after Waterloo no crisis or disaster (such as the unexpected difficulties in the First Afghan War or even the excitement generated during the invasion panics from the mid-1840s) resulted in more than relatively short-lived surges of activity – plus some increase in the number of soldiers. It was not until the Crimea that some significant changes were attempted.

Crisis management, 1823–30

The 1820s and 1830s provided several revealing examples of the strengths and weaknesses in the international position of the British. They found themselves isolated and helpless, for instance, in 1823 when the French chose to intervene and suppress a revolution in Spain. On the other hand, in 1826 troops and warships were sent to the Tagus as a tangible reminder that Portugal was a British preserve.

Canning, as Foreign Secretary, was also looking for ways to curb a new rival, the United States. The collapse of Spain's Latin American empire saw the British and Americans competing for trade and influence (see Document 4). It is true that both were anxious to deter any move by the continental European powers on behalf of Spain, but Canning's proposal in 1823 for a joint diplomatic stand was exploited by the Americans to set forth the principle of no further European colonisation in the New World. The claims made in the Monroe doctrine at the time, however, had no more substance than Canning's later boast in 1826 that through his Latin American policy he had called in the New World to redress the balance in the Old. The balance in the latter was unaffected, but in the New World the leaders of the new Latin American states fully appreciated that in the unlikely event of a European threat to the former colonies, the Royal Navy was the most effective deterrent and defence. In addition Britain's economic power – coupled with recognition of the new states – gave her the lion's share of most markets.

On the other hand, the British remained much more vulnerable in their own territories in North America. Attempts from 1815 onwards to devise a strategy for the defence of these colonies were thwarted by the lack of resources in relation to the extent of the area to be defended and the accelerating growth in the population and economic power of the United States. Furthermore, Britain had many and more important preoccupations elsewhere in the world. In effect the British could do little more than hope that they could deter an attack or buy time by putting what difficulties they could in the path of an American offensive into Canada. By way of a counter-offensive the Royal Navy could strike at American shipping and perhaps also at vulnerable coastal cities (though the mixed results at Washington, Baltimore and New Orleans in the War of 1812 were not entirely encouraging).

At the same time, as Liverpool and Castlereagh had already perceived, the best defence of British interests lay in patient diplomacy to avoid war – even at the cost of considerable concessions to the United States. The latter course was followed with some success by a Tory ministry under Peel between 1841 and 1846. Despite a war scare in 1845–6, the Webster–Ashburton treaty of 1842 was followed up by another agreement in June 1846 which completed the definition of the frontier between the United States and British North America to the Pacific. The British might have mourned some of their concessions, but these were offset by the possible avoidance of a war which they did not expect to win in the face of a really determined American assault. As it was, they were able to secure Vancouver Island where Esquimalt was later developed as a naval depot.[17] Even Palmerston resisted the temptation to try to draw advantage from America's war with Mexico in 1846–8.

The British had plenty to concern themselves with in Europe and the Near East down to 1856 without becoming embroiled with the United States. The revolt of the Greeks against their Turkish overlords in the 1820s threatened to have a major impact upon the balance of power in the Near East and the eastern Mediterranean, and this soon became the most serious test of British foreign and defence policy since 1815. The Greeks, after some initial success against the Turks, began to face disaster when Egyptian forces arrived to assist their nominal Turkish overlord. A Greek defeat, however, could not be countenanced by the Russians, yet intervention on their part was likely to threaten the future of the Ottoman Empire. In London, enhanced Russian influence at one end of the Mediterranean was expected to have adverse repercussions on

British interests there and elsewhere. From the time of Lous XIV, Britain had put a high value on naval command of that sea.

Canning decided in 1826 that Russia could best be influenced and restrained by an offer of diplomatic co-operation. He refused to be distracted by Russia's war with Persia (1826–8), despite the existence of an Anglo-Persian treaty relationship since 1801 and the possible value of Persia to the security of India. For Canning, the survival of the bulk of the Ottoman Empire was much more important. He did not want Russia to gobble Greece 'at one mouthful and Turkey at the next!' The answer, he believed, was to use 'every engine short of war . . . to save Greece through the agency of the Russian name upon the fears of Turkey'. Unfortunately the Turks refused to be intimidated by Anglo-Russian diplomacy, and were encouraged by Greek setbacks. In 1827 Britain and Russia, backed by France, decided to go a step further. They now tried through a combined display of naval power to impose an armistice in Greece.

A temporary Russian naval presence in the Mediterranean was seen by Canning as a lesser and more manageable evil than the advance of a Russian army towards Constantinople. Not everyone agreed. Lord Grey, though a friend to the Greeks, described a Russian fleet in the Mediterranean as a dangerous trespasser. As it turned out, the combined fleet's efforts to persuade the Turks and Egyptians to accept a cease-fire reached an unintended and bloody climax at the battle of Navarino. Nor did the allied victory – complete as it was – persuade the Turks to give way. Canning had died before the battle, and his successors were unsure what to do next. Wellington, as Prime Minister from 1828, was particularly dismayed, and was disposed to think that almost any action would make matters worse. Among his worries were the possible effects of an anti-Turkish policy on Britain's position in India.[18] Victories by the Russians in a war with Persia in 1828 gave them mastery of the Caspian and bases from which to move further south-eastward towards India.

Ostensibly Britain was friendless. Her fleet would be her only instrument of consequence in the first phase of any Near Eastern conflict. The French were clearly eager to take advantage of a highly fluid situation. Furthermore, Wellington and Aberdeen believed that a European war would be a disaster both politically and economically. The Duke, in a moment of deep pessimism, wrote in October 1829 that Turkey could not be saved. 'It is gone in fact: and the Tranquillity of the World . . . along with it.' Fortunately for him the Russians were counting the costs of the recent campaign. They had secured all they needed for the time being from Persia. The campaign of 1828–9 against the Turks, though ultimately successful, had been expensive. In due course a special committee concluded in St Petersburg in September 1829 that 'the advantages of the preservation of the Ottoman Empire outweigh its disadvantages'.

In time Wellington himself began to hope that common sense might prevail, and – in line with Castlereagh's earlier thinking – he looked to the Concert of Europe in some form or another to pick up the pieces. Overall, however, it was Aberdeen as Foreign Secretary rather than Wellington who (in the months following the Russo-Turkish Treaty of Adrianople of September 1829) tried to make the most of the diplomatic possibilities. Though already inclined to despair of the Turkish empire, he could see advantages in its temporary preservation. The effects of its collapse were likely to be felt from Greece to the Indus. Greece itself, however, could be treated as an exception, and here he was able to make a start to a policy which his successor (Lord Palmerston) took up, expanded and carried to a successful conclusion – namely, that Russian influence might best be constrained by the creation of a largish and independent Greece. The new state came into being in 1832, and – despite its faults – served British interests moderately well thereafter.[19]

But the government was also careful, even after the conclusion of peace between Russia and Turkey, to maintain a larger battlefleet in the Mediterranean than that of either France or Russia. The Admiralty was reasonably satisfied with the regional naval balance, despite the current French operations in Algiers. Ideally British interests also demanded that the fleet should have free access to the Black Sea. Relative strength at sea, however, could not conceal Britain's need for a major ally on land in the event of war.

Meanwhile a keen debate was developing over the degree and nature of the Russian threat to India and how this might be countered.[20] In 1829–30 Aberdeen and others were profoundly worried by the weakness of Turkey in Asia and by the recent victories of the Russians over Persia. Aberdeen himself wrote on 31 October 1829 that Russia could now control Asia Minor 'at her pleasure'. No serious obstacle existed to advances whether to east or west. The Sultan of Turkey, it seemed, would continue to 'reign only by the sufferance of Russia'. Yet what could Britain do? Some experts demanded strong action, such as the passage of the Mediterranean fleet through the Dardanelles to the Sea of Marmora or the incitement of the Persians to further resistance. Ellenborough, as president of the Board of Control, called for a 'world in arms' from Europe to Persia against Russia.

Colonel George de Lacy Evans was adding to the excitement with his two books, *On the Designs of Russia* (1828) and *On the Practicability of an Invasion of India* (1829). He argued that both the Turkish Straits and Central Asia were highly vulnerable to Russia. If the latter controlled the Straits, the British would be denied access to the Black Sea, and therefore to the theatre where they could most easily counter or divert the Russians from any drive into Central Asia. The best Russian line of advance to India, in his opinion, would be from the Black Sea to the Caspian and from thence to Khiva, the Oxus River and Kabul. India itself would then be in imminent danger.

By and large, however, Wellington and Aberdeen still believed that British India could be successfully defended against a Russian advance even to its very borders. The greater threat lay within India itself where a native rising might be encouraged simply by news of distant Russian successes. Finally, and as usual, both British and Indian interests demanded that any counter-strategy should be as inexpensive as possible. Thus, Wellington thought it possible to neutralise a Russian army of 30,000 which established itself temporarily in Kabul. Problems would arise only in the face of a longer challenge. This might require Britain not only to give financial aid to the Indian government but even, ultimately, to take action against Russia in Europe.

This matter was keenly discussed by others, notably by Ellenborough and British officials and soldiers in India. Nevertheless some of those who were most eager to take counter-action agreed that a major Russian threat was not imminent. The two empires were separated by some of the most difficult and inhospitable terrain in the world. But it was difficult not to worry in view of the obvious political and military weaknesses of the Muslim regimes in what – in theory – should have been buffer zones.

Within the cabinet itself Ellenborough was the most active promoter of what became known as the 'Great Game' in Asia between the British and the Russians – in short which power would exercise most influence or control in Persia, Afghanistan and Turkestan? Yet he too had to concede that the Russians for the time being were unlikely to attempt more than modest ventures, such as the incitement of Indian unrest against British rule. Time, however, was still precious, and the British should use it to create as invulnerable a position as possible in anticipation of any future challenge.

Edward Ingram contends that Ellenborough showed 'the truer perception of the needs of a continental state' (which Britain had become through her acquisition of an Indian empire) than Castlereagh and those who gave priority to the balance of power in Europe. In his view Britain had the easier task in Europe, given her insular position and her ability to exploit the divisions of the other powers. This understates the difficulties that Britain had faced – or it seemed possible that she might have to face in Europe. The outcome in the Near East might prove relevant both to the defence of India and to the great-power balance, while British access to the Black Sea (for whatever purposes – Asiatic or European) might be determined by current European power alignments.

It was, however, left to a new ministry under Lord Grey from the close of 1830 to grapple with these issues. This new Whig cabinet at first found much to preoccupy it at home and in Europe. Only later did its foreign minister, Palmerston, catch something of Ellenborough's enthusiasm for the Great Game, and even then he saw it as but part of a wider struggle for the defence of Britain's interests against Russia – in Europe and the Near East, as well as on the approaches to India.

In the fifteen years since the final overthrow of Napoleon, ministers had, despite some alarms, enjoyed reasonable success in their foreign policies. They had been helped by the fact that France, though restless both at home and abroad, had stopped far short of anything akin to Jacobinism or Bonapartism. Revolutionary unrest persisted in Europe, but it had not reached unmanageable proportions – although the future of Greece and Belgium had yet to be resolved. Admittedly Russia's activities in the Near East and Persia were compelling the British to pay closer attention to the region from the eastern Mediterranean to the approaches to India. Similarly, although Britain had enjoyed considerable success with the newly independent states of Latin America, she had reason to remain wary of the potential of the United States.

These years have given rise to a lengthy academic debate over the calibre of statesmanship displayed by Castlereagh and Canning, and the degree to which there was continuity or discontinuity in their foreign policies. Some consideration has also been given to the Wellington ministry, and whether its policies have been underrated. Castlereagh stands out as the most European-minded of British ministers, perhaps until Edward Heath in the 1970s. Canning emphatically dismissed his predecessor's enthusiasm for co-operation and close contacts with the leaders of the other great powers as a 'new and very questionable policy'. In addition, the two men differed sharply in personality and in their approach to politics. But account must also be taken of the circumstances at home and abroad. Castlereagh was given an unusually free hand by his cabinet colleagues, while in Europe he could exploit the post-war exhaustion and fear of new internal or international crises. Metternich trusted Castlereagh as much as he distrusted Canning.

Canning believed that Britain should follow a neutral course between the extremes of democracy and autocracy, whereas Castlereagh had leant towards autocracy to try to restrain and manipulate it where appropriate. Canning also needed to cultivate support in Parliament in order to weaken his critics in the cabinet. But while his public rhetoric carried hints of progressive sympathies, in reality his basic interpretation of British interests was as conservative as that of Castlereagh. Change, if change there had to be, should be orderly and in accord with British interests. He wished to limit the advance of French, Russian and American influence wherever possible. While formulating his own approach, he found, like Castlereagh, that the Russians might best be constrained by a policy of co-operation rather than direct opposition. Like Castlereagh, he was conscious of the British interest in peace and in low defence spending. As for his successors, while they might have lacked his oratorical gifts or the fertility of his mind, by 1830 their policies in the Near East were showing signs of promise. They were also refusing to succumb to the more alarmist views of some of the Indian specialists (see Document 5).

Palmerston: foreign policy and defence, 1830–38

British interest in Europe was sharpened in 1830 by a new surge of revolutionary unrest. It began in France with the overthrow of the

Bourbons, and soon spread to Belgium, Italy and Poland. Grey and Palmerston privately sympathised with the Poles in their revolt against the Russians, but knew that Britain could do no more than try to localise the crisis. Fortunately France seemed in no mood or condition to meddle, and in time the Polish revolt and the other upheavals in Europe tended to strengthen rather than weaken Britain's diplomatic hand. France (under the Orleanist monarchy brought to power by the July revolution) was isolated, and the eastern powers were preoccupied by Poland and apprehensive of revolution elsewhere. Each had occasion to court London.

The Belgian revolt against the Dutch highlighted both Britain's advantages and her weaknesses. A Dutch invasion of Belgium in the summer of 1831 had to be countered by French troops. The British navy was very much an observer able, perhaps, to exert some moral influence. Late in 1832 it blockaded the Dutch ports (to assist in the final expulsion of Dutch forces from Antwerp), but this operation was too brief to cause real pain. It is true that the expansion of the British fleet from the beginning of 1831 was an important signal of intent, and Palmerston made the most of this, especially in his dealings with France. But above all he was able to capitalise on France's acute sense of isolation, as the three eastern powers continued to treat the Orleanist constitutional monarchy as a centre of subversion. The Austrian Chancellor in 1831 even seemed prepared to contemplate military action against France, until he was reminded of the empire's financial predicament. Austrian weakness was also reflected in the appeal to London in April 1831 for a display of British naval power in the Mediterranean to discourage the French from meddling in the political troubles of Italy. Around the same time Palmerston was confidently observing that, with six sail-of-the-line in that sea, the British could do what they liked with any French fleet.

Meanwhile, over Belgium Palmerston firmly warned Paris on 16 August 1831 that Britain would not tolerate the establishment of any separate influence in Brussels. The French, he intimated, would face 'a war with all the rest of the world' in which Britain would ruin them at sea, while the eastern powers would combine to crush the Poles before joining in the conflict (presumably supported if necessary by British subsidies).[21]

At the same time, although the eastern powers continued to sympathise with the Dutch, he calculated that they would not risk war with Britain and France. The Belgian question was not finally resolved until 1839. The outcome, however, was very much more in accord with the interests and wishes of Britain than of any other power. Yet most of the straw for the bricks which Palmerston had so skilfully manufactured had been supplied by others.

The problems of the Iberian peninsula in the 1830s proved less tractable. Ostensibly Britain was involved in a struggle between autocratic and constitutional dynastic factions in Portugal and later in Spain. In co-operation with France, she helped to uphold the 'liberal' cause against the reactionary eastern powers. Whig rhetoric made much of the political principles which were said to be at stake. The ideological aspect was also emphasised by Lord Aberdeen – but in his case from a Tory point of view. Thus he welcomed the establishment of a firm alignment between Russia and Austria in 1833, since this offered 'the best prospect of arresting the progress of revolution in Europe'. He also favoured a policy of strict British non-intervention in the Iberian peninsula. Up to a point this view might seem to have been vindicated, when later Spanish conduct so often failed to conform to Palmerston's hopes and expectations.

But Palmerston's thinking with respect to Iberia was also much influenced by wider considerations. Irrespective of political principles, he saw Russia as an ambitious and expanding great power. He was particularly disturbed by Russia's apparent gains in the Near East as a result of the Treaty of Unkiar Skelessi which had been concluded with the Turks in 1833. The Tsar had seemingly made himself the protector of the Ottoman Empire. The meeting of Nicholas I and Metternich at Münchengrätz in September 1833 (with Prussia joining the combination a month later) increased the Foreign Secretary's fears of a powerful united absolutist alliance. He was determined to deny further successes to the eastern trio, and to reverse any impression that the overall balance in Europe was moving eastward – especially to the advantage of Russia. Iberia therefore became the natural arena for a complicated power struggle as Portuguese and Spanish 'absolutists' rallied behind Dom Miguel and Don Carlos against the constitutional monarchists (see Document 6).

France was once again the obvious partner of Britain, though with the qualification that she should not be allowed to gain any exclusive influence in Iberia. In Portugal it was relatively easy to secure the upper hand against all comers, especially given the many weaknesses within the Miguelist faction. The struggle inside Spain was fiercer and more protracted. It was also complicated by the ongoing Anglo-French competition for favours in Madrid. Once again the British profited from the fear in Paris of hostile action by the eastern powers if France showed signs of sending an army into Spain.[22] Many Frenchmen also recalled the guerrilla war in Spain from 1808, rather than their own successful intervention in 1823. In the end only token British and French forces were sent to Spain, but they too contributed to the dissension between 'friends'.

If the Carlist war proved to be an extremely messy conflict both politically and militarily, the British were at least able to achieve their minimum objectives and to do so at no great cost to themselves. A few warships (and their marines) were usefully employed along disputed parts of the Spanish coast. Some British volunteers served with the 'liberals'. It is true that Spain, following the defeat of the Carlists, did not become a model constitutional state, nor was French influence permanently excluded. But in the wider context of power politics, Palmerston had served a reminder that Britain was a force to be reckoned with in the right circumstances. If he had fallen short in the realisation of his own objectives, the eastern powers had been unable to make an impressive showing.

Indeed, Palmerston might have been sufficiently forceful in Spain to persuade others to take more account of Britain in the Near East by the end of the decade (see below, pp. 40–2). That region had been troubling him increasingly since 1833, by which time the Russians had become the leading foreign influence in Constantinople. This was the result of a war between the Turks and Mehemet Ali of Egypt. In November 1831 the latter had launched a great offensive through Syria against his Turkish overlord. His forces a year later were within striking distance of Constantinople. When London failed to respond to the frantic appeals from the Porte for assistance, the Turks turned to St Petersburg. In February 1833 a Russian squadron passed through the Bosphorus to defend Turkey in Europe from the Egyptians. Meanwhile British naval commitments elsewhere – as well as the failure to anticipate the character and scale of the Russian involvement – had delayed the strengthening of the Mediterranean fleet (to seven ships-of-the-line) until April 1833.[23]

The Russians made the most of their advantage to write into the

Treaty of Unkiar Skelessi of July 1833 a clause which required the Turks to close the Dardanelles to any foreign powers at war with Russia. The Russians were obviously anxious to exclude the Royal Navy (perhaps in alliance with that of France) from the Black Sea. The treaty, as conceived in 1833, was a defensive move. The British, however, suspected something more sinister, and – irrespective of the wording of any clause relating to the Straits – feared that the Ottoman Empire was becoming a dependency of Russia. Even if the latter's current aims were limited and defensive, circumstances and objectives could always change, especially with the continued building of ships for Russia's Black Sea fleet. Furthermore, any alterations to the balance of power in the Near East might have implications for the safety of British interests in India and bordering regions. Palmerston, for instance, was already beginning to emphasise the strategic importance of the Central Asian khanate of Khiva.

The close alignment of Russia with Austria and Prussia from the autumn of 1833 further inflamed Palmerston's fears that a grand design was being devised in St Petersburg. He saw Russian policy in Europe and Asia as intimately linked.[24] If Britain was vulnerable in either Europe or Asia, Russia might be expected to try to exploit such weakness, either to secure advantages in the region under threat, or to improve her leverage in the other. The great expansion of the Russian Baltic fleet during the 1830s was a further source of concern to many in London. In any case Russophobia was already rampant among those who detested all autocrats – especially after the crushing of the Polish revolt.

David Gillard raises the interesting question: 'how often does international conflict arise from illusion and misunderstanding as to an opponent's intentions?' He offers no straightforward answer with regard to Anglo-Russian relations at this time. On the one hand, he points out that enough is now known of Russian thinking in the early 1830s to conclude that no more than a consolidation of Russia's position in Asia was intended. Dread of revolution in Europe was the main preoccupation. On the other, he sets out the difficulties which arise once one considers the longer term. Here the British had more reason to fear that Russia would in time become too strong and its Asiatic neighbours too weak for the status quo to be preserved. Ambition might feed on opportunities, just as priorities or personalities might change in St Petersburg. Britain herself had so much at stake in India that it would have seemed the height of foolishness not to have taken precautions. Yet there was always the danger that defensive measures might provoke the very action they were intended to deter.[25]

The British, in practice, soon discovered diplomatic openings in Constantinople. The Sultan had no wish to remain a mere satrap of the Tsar. Palmerston also hoped that, through internal reform, the Ottoman Empire might acquire new strength and vitality, and become more resistant to Russian influence. In particular the British were able to improve their own commercial prospects in 1838 when the Sultan agreed to a new treaty based on the hope (incorrect) that the British would help him recover the extensive territories lost to the Egyptians in 1831–3. Britain's bargaining power was also enhanced by her Mediterranean fleet, or, as Palmerston noted, its 'moral effects . . . and the *uncertainty*' which it created in the minds of others, thus preventing 'the necessity of its having to act by force of arms'. The fleet certainly alarmed the Russians, who still feared a British naval *coup* in the Dardanelles. Their own efforts to create a force with which to seize Constantinople had made relatively little progress as late as 1841.[26]

By the late 1830s, however, much more seemed at stake than the future of the Ottoman Empire. The British were having to play several chess games simultaneously, games which had a habit of running into each other. While their position was perhaps improving in the eastern Mediterranean, British diplomats in Persia were clearly at a disadvantage in competition with the Russians. The Shah's main objective was the recovery of the disputed city of Herat from the Afghans, an objective which the Russians happily encouraged. Herat lay on one of the main routes into north-west India, and its control by a ruler who leant towards Russia could not be tolerated by the British. Furthermore, if Herat fell to Persia, this might intensify the political divisions within Afghanistan and so add to the instability and vulnerability of that country. From this it was but a short step to fearful imaginings of trouble in Afghanistan having repercussions in the Punjab in India, a region which in its turn was in conflict with Sind. There was no knowing where the rot might spread to the detriment of British interests in the sub-continent.[27]

British policy-makers continued to explore various possibilities. Hopes persisted that the growth of British commerce would help to draw the rulers of Persia, Central Asia and north-west India under the shadow of British power. It might also help to create a more stable and progressive environment, which in itself would provide a more formidable barrier to Russia. Overall it was hoped that local peoples would be encouraged to incline spontaneously towards the more *progressive* imperial power. But such calculations under-estimated the continuing obsession of the region's rulers with old land disputes and their faith in the persuasive powers of armed men. Indeed, the British themselves relied heavily on their old mili-tary ally, Ranjit Singh of the Punjab – a tie which in its turn helped to obstruct a deal with Dost Mohammed, the ruler in the central city of Afghanistan, Kabul.

Given such a tangle of regional divisions, it is difficult to be wholly convinced by any of the varied strategies which were being canvassed by the experts in the 1830s. Each was supposed to give Britain an assured protective barrier against Russia – a barrier made up of friendly or neutral states from the north-west of India, through Afghanistan and Persia and on to Baghdad and the Persian Gulf. But the unravelling of one regional tangle only seemed to tighten the knots elsewhere. Sir Charles Metcalfe, one experienced Indian administrator, concluded that Britain should content herself with a defensive frontier along the Sutlej River and consolidate the alliance with the Punjab – even at the expense of relations with Sind and the Afghans.

Palmerston and a new Governor-General. Lord Auckland, how-ever, independently reached the conclusion that it was too danger-ous to put one's faith in a single ally. They ambitiously set out to resolve the rivalries between the Punjab, Sind and Afghanistan. Unfortunately, by 1838 this strategy was being undermined by the growing pro-Russian sympathies of Dost Mahommed in Kabul as he pursued his old quarrels with the Punjab. The Afghan princes in Kandahar were also leaning towards Russia. Persia continued to pose problems. Further north, Khiva and Bokhara seemed under threat from Russia.

In addition, account had to be taken of the southward expansion of Mehemet Ali's Egypt. Palmerston declared that Britain would not tolerate an Egyptian presence in the Persian Gulf or at Aden (in practice this particular problem was soon settled by the British occupation of Aden in January 1839 to safeguard the developing steamer connection between Bombay and Suez). But in the north there existed the growing danger of a new war between the Sultan and Egypt. This threatened to confirm Russian influence in Constantinople. Britain, it seemed, had to nerve herself to take bold decisions simultaneously in the Great Game and the Near Eastern Question. Palmerston and others, with very different degrees of confidence, prepared to act.

It is difficult to know how highly Palmerston rated the power of Russia. His references to its strength or weaknesses seem to have been much influenced by his momentary tactical needs. Certainly he would sometimes belittle an opponent in order to persuade more cautious colleagues to accept a bold policy of bluff. In 1835 – in contrast to his expressed fears in 1833 – he was jauntily describing Russia as a great humbug. A single British campaign could reverse her progress by half a century (and at times during the Crimean War he really seemed to believe that Russia could be compelled to give up many of the territorial gains made in Europe and the region of the Black Sea since the late eighteenth century). In similar vein he argued that Russia preferred to advance by 'encroachment'. If firmly resisted, she would pause and wait for a better opportunity.

At the same time he recognised that Britain could not be strong everywhere, and that there were limits to what could be spent on defence in ordinary times. Although Melbourne as Prime Minister in the late 1830s agreed that the peacetime fleet should always be large enough to serve as the nucleus for rapid expansion, he also declared that forever to be making great military preparations was almost as bad as living in a state of war itself. Palmerston's reactions to such constraints were to remind foreign powers continually not to judge Britain by her naval or military power in being, but by what she could mobilise (and provide by way of subsidies to allies) in the event of war. One of the best ways to demonstrate this was by summoning up strong parliamentary and popular support at the appropriate moment. He told Melbourne in 1835, 'Expose her [Russia's] plans, and you half defeat them. Raise public opinion against her and you double her difficulties.' A sequence of budget deficits in the late 1830s proved less inhibiting than might have been expected because the Tory opposition joined in the demands for more defence spending. Palmerston at one point was talking of quick success in Afghanistan while the Russian Baltic fleet was frozen in during the winter of 1838–9.[28]

Palmerston in these years was obviously a subscriber to the belief that fortune favoured the brave. Perhaps deep down he reasoned that it was less dangerous to appear self-confident and assertive than to be guided by a less optimistic – possibly even a more objective – calculation of the odds. Britain might succeed more cheaply (or might be able to succeed only) by some degree of bluff. At worst it should always be possible to find some means to cover one's retreat. Nor was his approach invariably belligerent or admonitory. He recognised that if Britain had no permanent friends or enemies, she needed friends in proportion to her enemies at any one time. And neither did he always ignore the concert of Europe. But in practice, for most of the 1830s he had to depend on the French 'alliance' in Europe and the Near East – however much it grieved him to have to tolerate the 'little ebullitions of [French] national conceit'. At this time, too, he was having to tread carefully in his dealings with the United States. Diplomacy and tact, as much as reinforcements to Canada, were needed as the British tried to send the right signals to Washington.[29] Meanwhile, a totally unexpected shift of thinking in St Petersburg was about to enable him to seize the initiative in dramatic fashion in the Near East.

Notes

1   C. J. Bartlett, *Castlereagh*, London, 1966, pp. 130–1.

2   Bartlett, *Castlereagh*, pp. 121–3.

3   G. J. Marcus, *The Age of Nelson: the Royal Navy 1783–1815*, New York, 1971, pp. 407–9, and for more detail see A. N. Ryan (ed.), *The Saumarez Papers 1808–12*, London, 1968.

4   Sir C. K. Webster, *British Diplomacy, 1813–15: select documents dealing with the reconstruction of Europe*, London, 1921, p. 317.

5   M. E. Yapp, *Strategies of British India: Britain, Iran and Afghanistan, 1798–1850*, Oxford, 1980, pp. 4–19.

6   Kenneth Bourne, *Britain and the Balance of Power in North America, 1815–1908*, London, 1967, pp. 7–8.

7   Bartlett, *Castlereagh*, chapter 7.

8   K. Bourne, *Palmerston: the early years, 1784–1841*, London, 1982, p. 134.

9   Michael S. Partridge, *Military Planning for the Defence of the United Kingdom, 1814–70*, London, 1989, p. 46.

10   C. J. Bartlett, *Great Britain and Sea Power, 1815–53*, Oxford, 1963, pp. 23–6, 125.

11 Bartlett, *Sea Power*, pp. 214–15; K. Bourne and D. C. Watt (eds.), *Studies in International History*, London, 1967, p. 191.

12 Bourne and Watt, *Studies*, pp. 199–200, 204.

13 Partridge, *Military Planning*, pp. 66–71.

14 David French, *The British Way in Warfare, 1688–2000*, London, 1990, pp. 124–5; Ian W. F. Beckett and J. Gooch (eds.), *Politicians and Defence*, Manchester, 1981, p. 9.

15 Bartlett, *Sea Power*, pp. 323–9.

16 Partridge, *Military Planning*, chapter 3. See also M. Partridge, 'Wellington and the defence of the realm, 1819–52', chapter 12 in N. Gash (ed.), *Wellington: studies in the military and political career of the first Duke of Wellington*, Manchester, 1990; and Hew Strachan, *Wellington's Legacy: the reform of the British Army, 1830–54*, Manchester, 1984.

17 Bourne, *North America*, pp. 93–169.

18 Edward Ingram, *The Beginning of the Great Game in Asia, 1828–34*, Oxford, 1979, pp. 40–1, 48.

19 Muriel E. Chamberlain, *Lord Aberdeen*, London and New York, 1983, pp. 220–5.

20 Ingram, *Great Game*, pp. 50–84; David Gillard, *The Struggle for Asia: a study in British and Russian Imperialism*, London, 1977, pp. 30–3.

21 Kenneth Bourne, *The Foreign Policy of Victorian England, 1830–1902*, p. 220.

22 Alan Sked (ed.), *Europe's Balance of Power, 1815–48*, London, 1979, pp. 68–75.

23 Gillard, *Asia*, pp. 34–8; Bartlett, *See Power*, pp. 89–93.

24 Gillard, *Asia*, p. 38; Bourne, *Palmerston*, p. 559.

25 Gillard, *Asia*, pp. 39–42.

26 Bartlett, *Sea Power*, pp. 107, 119–20; see also J. C. Daly, *Russian Sea Power and 'the Near Eastern Question', 1827–41*, London, 1991, for a study of the limitations of Russian naval power for geographical, economic and other reasons. The British were unduly alarmist.

27 Gillard, *Asia*, pp. 46–52. For added detail see Yapp, *Strategies*, pp. 114–50, 241–303.

28 Bartlett, *Sea Power*, pp. 120, 122–5.

29 Bourne, *North America*, pp. 75–93.

2

No permanent
friends or enemies
1839–56

Afghanistan and the Near East, 1839–44

In the years between 1839 and 1856 Britain was remarkably successful in working with either France or Russia to promote her interests
at the expense of the other, or simply in exploiting the gulf which
separated those two powers. In 1839–41, for instance, the rivalry
which had dominated Anglo-Russian relations for most of the 1830s
was suddenly replaced by a selective friendship. Indeed, by 1840
so much had changed that Palmerston was briefly poised to risk
war on the side of Russia against France. Yet this partnership with
Russia in the Near East did not preclude continuing British competition with the same power in Central Asia as long as Palmerston
remained in office. Similarly, even when the British were allied with
France against Russia in the Crimean War (1854–6) they continued
to keep a wary eye on their partner's ambitions and activities. Relations began to deteriorate with Paris as soon as peace was concluded with Russia.

In 1838 Palmerston had no inkling that a selective partnership
with Russia was just around the corner when he began to encourage action against Dost Mahommed in Kabul. Nor would such
knowledge necessarily have changed his policy had he known. He
was convinced that Britain could not compete successfully for influence in Persia. He was therefore all the more determined to act in
Afghanistan, a region where he believed the British might have a
real chance of prevailing over the Russians. Afghanistan was in any
case, for him, just one theatre in the wider struggle with Russia

which ran from Europe to India.[1] In contrast, those who governed India were more anxious to impress the peoples of the sub-continent with their ability to vanquish any threat – external or internal – to British pre-eminence in India.

Unfortunately, knowledge in London of 'the Centre of Asia' was imperfect, or – as Lord Salisbury remarked during a later crisis – people relied too much on small-scale maps. Good information on the nature of Afghan society and politics was vital, as well as on the problems of campaigning in that remote country. Too much of the intelligence which reached London came from interested and prejudiced parties. Success in this particular arena of the Great Game was, in any case, likely to prove elusive at best. Factionalism and fighting seemed as natural as breathing to the Afghan tribes-men. In that inhospitable terrain, small armies were defeated and large armies starved (unless well served by secure supply lines). Wellington had the insight to see that intervention would not be conclusive – it would mean a 'perennial march into Afghanistan'.

Nevertheless, all seemed to go well at first with the military operations. The invading army speedily established a puppet in Kabul in August 1839. The Russians remained quiet – they had more important matters on their mind. Only later did the exorbitant cost of trying to sustain British influence and the new client regime become apparent. The resources of north-west India were sorely strained by the demands of the military. There were too few animals to support both a campaign and the local economy. These and other lessons, however, were learned only in the course of the war (1838–42).

By comparison, Palmerston's grasp of realities in the concurrent Near Eastern crisis was impressive, once the various participants showed their hands. At first, as matters threatened to come to a head between the Sultan and the Egyptians, Palmerston was still intent upon denying the Russians a second triumph on the lines of that achieved in 1833. He made much of the dispatch of a fleet to Constantinople at the critical moment. This, he claimed, 'of itself would be checkmate to Russia'. Such a venture, he reflected, might or might not be attempted in partnership with France. He also looked to naval power to deter the Egyptians from making a bid for independence from the Porte.

But he began to revise his calculations when it was the Turks, not the Egyptians, who precipitated the crisis. Worse, the Turks, having begun a war in April 1839, proceeded to lose it in a most spectacular fashion. Although the five great powers drew together to try to control the situation, they did so in an atmosphere of mutual distrust. Palmerston's leaning towards France was based on need, not confidence in his partner's intentions. He was therefore willing to give the Russians a hearing when – from September 1839 – they began to come up with radical new proposals. These sprang from their worries over unrest in the Caucasus, their current financial problems, and the Tsar's belated realisation that his ambitious naval programmes in the Baltic and Black Seas (especially the latter) were not providing him with the expected bargaining power. Nor had the Treaty of Unkiar Skelessi bound the Porte to Russia as tightly as expected. Finally, Nicholas I feared that unless he acted first he might find himself confronted by a hostile combination made up of France, Britain and perhaps Austria. At least one of the three had to be detached. An overture to Britain made a great deal of sense.[2]

Nicholas would have no truck with the upstart and 'revolutionary' Orleanist dynasty in France. Nor was he on good terms with Metternich at this time. In any case, there was much to be said for wooing the leading naval power in order to end its 'liberal *entente*' with the French. Proposals were therefore sent to London for concerted action to protect the Sultan against the Egyptians. In return, the Tsar required British help to negotiate a European agreement which would close the Straits to all warships. Given the limited power of the Russian Black Sea fleet and the dubious value of the 1833 treaty, this seemed much the best way forward. Russia needed a viable Ottoman Empire and a secure position for itself in the Black Sea. But such a policy needed British help. It was not long before Palmerston began to see advantages for his own strategy in these propositions.

His biggest problem at first was to persuade cabinet colleagues to exchange 'liberal' France for 'autocratic' Russia, and to recognise that Russian ambitions could best be restrained by a policy of co-operation with St Petersburg (a revival of the strategy of Canning in the Greek question). Palmerston was also intent – to the point of resignation – upon the revival of the Ottoman Empire, notably by re-establishing the Turks in Syria (see Document 7). To that end he was willing to risk conflict with Egypt and, if necessary, with France. By way of justification, he argued that a strong Egypt would always tend to align itself with France to the detriment of British interests in the eastern Mediterranean. As a final bonus he claimed that a stronger Ottoman Empire would be less susceptible to Russian influence.

Palmerston refused to be impressed or deterred by French opposition. France, he insisted, was unlikely to risk war. There were no longer so many Frenchmen who saw this as the best road to fame and fortune. But his ensuing difficulties with his colleagues demonstrate how easily the British government could have come to a very different decision. Some ministers and naval officers also wondered if Palmerston's objectives were as easily attainable as he suggested. Their nervousness increased as matters moved to a climax in the autumn of 1840 when British naval forces were faced by a superior French squadron in the eastern Mediterranean (Document 8). Nor were the sceptics persuaded – even if the French held their hand – that the allies (the British, Turks, Russians and Austrians) had sufficient forces to guarantee the speedy expulsion of the Egyptians from Syria.[3]

Furthermore, this venture was being prepared at a time when British forces were already involved in China and Afghanistan. Problems persisted with the United States in North America. But Palmerston continued to argue that with sufficient determination all would be well. The French must be made to see that any naval advantage they enjoyed could be no more than temporary. In addition he made much of the support from Russia and Austria. A fortuitous bonus was provided by French bluster which prompted Prussia to look to the defence of the Rhine.

The Syrian campaign also went well. Acre, the chief Egyptian stronghold, fell with unexpected ease, thanks in part to a lucky shot which set off the main magazine. Sir Charles Webster, for all his praise of Palmerston's overall policy, concedes that the attack was 'amazingly successful'. It guaranteed the expulsion of the Egyptians from Syria. It also did so in a way and at a pace which left the diplomatic initiative very much in British hands. Palmerston therefore set out to try to consolidate the Ottoman Empire to the advantage of Britain. Russian demands for the closure of the Straits might have been a little unfortunate, but at least this was now to be arranged through an international (not a bilateral Russo-Turkish) agreement. Palmerston argued that Russia's gains at the Straits would be more than offset by the exclusion of its Black Sea fleet from the Mediterranean. (As he doubtless surmised, in times of crisis clauses governing the use or non-use of the Straits might not greatly influence the course of events.)

Palmerston needlessly continued to humiliate France even after he had secured his essential objectives. On the other hand he declined an appeal from the Tsar to join a permanent four-power alliance directed against that country. Britain, he replied, could be counted on to defend the balance in Europe when occasion demanded. He was determined not to limit Britain's freedom of action. In the improbable event of a Franco-Russian alignment, he claimed in private that Britain could always form a counterpoise with the Germanic powers. If in this whole crisis Palmerston had been dealt many strong cards by the other players, he had shown himself a formidable practitioner of *realpolitik*.

Meanwhile, this selective co-operation with Russia in the Near East had in no way inhibited British operations in Afghanistan. The British were assisted by the modest Central Asian objectives of the Tsar and his foreign minister. Indeed, Palmerston might have missed an opportunity in 1839 to define the respective limits of the two empires in Central Asia, and so improve the security of India by agreement. But, as Professor Yapp argues, Palmerston believed no treaty to be inviolable. He insisted that 'it was inevitable that a European power would be tempted to upset an Asian agreement in order to bring about a situation in Asia which could influence a European negotiation'. He, for his part, was determined to secure that option for Britain. With sufficient influence in Turkestan, he believed it would be possible not only to protect India from Russia, but to exert pressure on Russia elsewhere. But if a degree of scepticism concerning the value of any Central Asian treaty was appropriate, his own policy in Afghanistan was a failure. That turbulent country was not brought under British influence, let alone turned into a springboard to territories further north.[4]

The British client ruler in Kabul faced more and more revolts. A British force attempting to retreat to India in 1841 was eliminated – save for one survivor. Wellington was now among those to insist on vigorous action to regain the nation's 'Reputation in the East' from Constantinople to Peking (the First China War was still in progress). The armies of India duly took their revenge, yet in 1843 the British had to accept the return to power in Kabul of Dost Mahommed, the ruler they had overthrown in 1839. At great cost to the Indian economy (some £20 million and 50,000 camels) the British had proved that they could injure Afghanistan but not control it at tolerable expense to themselves. Even the impression made by their victory and temporary occupation lessened over time. The British had also given useful arguments to those Russians who favoured expansion in Asia – and especially towards India.[5]

From 1842 a new British government (under Sir Robert Peel) began to implement its preferred and more economical policy of consolidating British India along the line of the Indus. It also looked for ways to co-exist with the Russian empire. The Tsar's visit to Britain in 1844 marked the climax of this *détente*. But it was more a product of Russian than British diplomacy. Nicholas I continued to be primarily interested in Russian security in the Black Sea, in the future of the Ottoman Empire, and in the suppression of all revolutionary threats in Europe. Adventures in the Caspian region and Central Asia were less to his liking. Certainly it was Europe and more especially the Ottoman Empire which filled the Tsar's mind during his visit to Britain in 1844.

On the face of it, with Anglo-French relations in a poor state, he had chosen a good time. But Aberdeen, like Palmerston before him, did not wish to have his hands tied either against France or in the Near East where Russia might yet prove too aggressive. Perhaps there was also an unspoken assumption at work – namely, that the successors of Nicholas I and Nesselrode might select different priorities. True, the talks produced a memorandum which, from the British point of view, seemed to demonstrate Russia's desire to preserve the Ottoman Empire. But the Tsar, unfortunately, attached particular weight to the reference to concerted action by the two powers whenever the future of that empire seemed in doubt.[6] The British ministers, however, did not see the memorandum as constituting a commitment on their part. Thus were sown some of the seeds of the Crimean War.

France and the invasion panics, 1844–52

In the 1840s technological change began to have major effects on British defence thinking. In the south of England alone there were rail links from London to Harwich, Dover, Brighton, Portsmouth, Southampton and Tor Bay. By 1848 the telegraph was connecting London with Edinburgh, Leeds and Manchester in the north, and

Ipswich, Yarmouth, Portsmouth and Southampton in the south. The steamship (in its own right) and fully-rigged ships fitted with auxiliary engines were being introduced in growing numbers. Engine power, reliability and efficiency were improving. If the Admiralty was unimpressed by experiments with iron hulls, there was mounting interest in the screw propellor as a replacement for the paddle wheel in certain types of ship. With the screw – albeit as an auxiliary to sail – it was possible to think of mounting a full broadside of guns and to use such vessels as true ocean-going warships. So rapid was the advance of steam that at the Spithead review of August 1853 all but three of the forty ships present were fitted with engines, however small.[7]

At the same time, with the advent of steam power, Britain's island security appeared to be under threat. Steamships, it was feared, might facilitate surprise raids by an enemy, or even an invasion attempt across the English Channel. Troops might be moved with such speed and secrecy into northern France by railway and embarked in steamers that the defenders would have insufficient time in which to react. Steamships might even be able to elude such British warships as were at sea. A pamphlet written by the Prince de Joinville, the sailor son of the French king, added to the alarm. In 1844 he claimed (doubtless more with an eye to pleading his case in France than to frightening the British) that Napoleon in 1805, with only a few steamers, could have conveyed up to 20,000 troops across the Channel. He further contended that in the new age of steam France would be better placed to compete with the Royal Navy. Admittedly he also conceded that British steamers would pose serious threats to the coasts of France and to sea communications with her new colony in Algiers. But these qualifications impressed few British readers, especially when an Anglo-French dispute over Tahiti developed into a war scare in the summer of 1844.

Wellington and Palmerston led the demands for action. But leading Whigs and Tories – as well as generals and admirals – were soon in agreement that urgent action was required on land and at sea to improve national security. Lord John Russell as Prime Minister from 1846, for instance, suggested that 30,000 or 40,000 French soldiers might land and make a sudden march on London. His First Lord of the Admiralty asserted that the nation could not be regarded 'as safe' unless it could 'collect at very short notice large bodies of men well trained in arms'. Others, though equally anxious, contended that more ships (not soldiers) were the proper answer.[8] Only later was more notice given to the difficulties of assembling and dispatching a surprise invasion force.

The alarm shown by Peel's cabinet in 1844–6 was particularly revealing. It had inherited a sequence of budget deficits from the preceding ministry in 1841, and since then it had been trying to relax international tension wherever possible. Significant cuts were made to the service estimates in 1842 and 1843. Unfortunately not all Anglo-French differences had been resolved. Lord Aberdeen, the Foreign Secretary, agreed that France was the country most likely to disturb the peace. But his own response to Joinville and Tahiti was to work even harder for better relations with Paris. He even persuaded the Admiralty to allow the French an advantage of two ships-of-line in the Mediterranean – the converse of Palmerston's preference for superior strength. Nevertheless, British warships were twice sent to show the flag in Barcelona and give moral support to an anti-French government in Madrid. Other disputes were not long in coming, and in combination with the invasion scare these pushed up defence spending. Aberdeen vainly protested that such precautionary steps might precipitate the very conflict they were designed to prevent.

Wellington continued to insist that between 5,000 and 10,000 British troops might find themselves facing an invading force of up to 50,000 Frenchmen. Britain needed more regular soldiers. Demands for reform and expansion of the auxiliary forces soon followed. The sense of vulnerability inevitably revived interest in fortifications, both for defence of the navy's dockyards and for wider national defensive purposes. Wellington paid special attention to the security of south-eastern England as a whole. He was impressed by the military potential of the railways. London was the heart of the growing network, and should therefore be the main assembly point from which to deploy troops. His energy belied his years. Yet everything he attempted only highlighted the need for just the sort of institutionalised staff which he so bitterly opposed. Only with such experts could the new strategic and technical problems be evaluated in detail and from a variety of angles.[9]

Peel's own distrust of France now exceeded his desire to save money. He agreed in 1845 that Britain ought 'even in the midst of peace to be at ease upon vital points'.[10] Aberdeen's arguments carried less and less weight. Nor was Wellington impressed when he suggested that if the worst came to the worst, France would soon find herself opposed by the three eastern powers. They, remarked the Duke dismissively, had often proved broken reeds in the wars between 1793 and 1815.[11]

The succeeding Whig administration was equally concerned and active – especially with Palmerston as Foreign Secretary to jolly it along whenever it showed signs of faltering. Others supported him – not least the Prime Minister (see Documents 9 and 10). But there was unexpected relief in 1848 when the Orleanist monarchy was suddenly overthrown. It was soon evident that the new republican government in Paris had too much to preoccupy it at home to assert itself abroad. There were pressing economic and political reasons at home for the British government to economise, which it did promptly in the summer of 1848 to the dismay of the First Lord of the Admiralty. Russell even went so far in the Commons as to question the need for a strict interpretation of the two-power standard. But he was more nervous in private, and watched the French closely. The year 1849 found him reflecting on the importance of the Mediterranean fleet. This was needed to 'guard Malta, Corfu and Gibraltar, protect our interests in Italy, Turkey and Greece; and save us from the new French colony of Algeria.'[12]

There was also scope for diplomacy, and – in Palmerston's case – for foreign affairs to be used to win popularity at home as well as to exert influence abroad. He hoped, during the 'year of revolutions' (1848–9) to impress progressive opinion with his careful and selective championship of liberalism and nationalism. In practice, however, his influence on events was less than many believed or he would have liked. He was, for instance, unable to prevent the restoration of Austrian power in Italy in 1849 (where he would have welcomed a strengthened Piedmont in the north as a barrier to French interference). Nor, in the end, could his diplomacy and the temporary presence of some British warships save the Sicilian rebels from the wrath of the king in Naples. The fleet did better in the autumn of 1849 when it gave the Turks moral support against Austrian and Russian demands for the surrender of Hungarian refugees who had fled after a bitter struggle in the Habsburg Empire.

Palmerston displayed particular shrewdness in his dealings with France. As Louis Napoleon Bonaparte gradually emerged as the key figure in the confused politics which followed the French Revolution of February 1848, so Palmerston was careful to cultivate his favour where possible. Thus he responded favourably to Louis Napoleon's *coup d'état* in December 1851 (Document 11), which completed the first stage of the latter's rise to power. This gesture, however, dismayed many in Britain who recalled the Napoleonic Wars, or who were outraged by this blow against progressive politics in France. This might not have mattered in itself, but there were ministerial colleagues whose patience had been tried for far too long by Palmerston's determination to treat foreign policy as his own exclusive preserve. They were able to use the unpopularity of his approval of the Bonapartist *coup* to drive him from office.

But it is important to note that there were other politicians who shared his views and quietly regretted the current violence of the British press against the French President. Lord Ellenborough, for instance, thought that if the nation were unprepared to pay for adequate defences, it would do well to treat a near and powerful neighbour less offensively. Nevertheless, time would show that not even alliance with France in the Crimean War could dispel this fundamental national distrust of a Bonaparte for long.

Not surprisingly, the triumph of Louis Napoleon was soon followed by increases in the service estimates as anti-French excitement spread in Britain. Work proceeded on fortifications for the dockyards, while the creation of a militia was seen as a matter of urgency to reinforce the regular army at home. It was controversy over legislation for this force which gave Palmerston his chance to join in a heterogeneous political alliance to overthrow his former cabinet colleagues in February 1852. The creation of the militia was thus left to a new Tory ministry. The resulting force of 80,000 militiamen proved its value as early as the Crimean War when it freed regulars from garrison duties at home, and also provided 30,000 volunteers for the army.

The scares with France were real, but they were also used by various ministers to try to correct some of the basic deficiencies in the armed forces. Changes included a steady expansion in the number of troops at home after the realisation in the mid-1840s that, once the key points in Britain had been garrisoned, the nation would be lucky if it could put 10,000 troops in the field against an invader. Ministers at their most sanguine also reasoned that it did no harm for the French to see that Britain was on the alert.

Meanwhile, the Admiralty from 1849 was considering how best to deploy its main warships to maximise national security. At first it was thought that a large fleet in the Mediterranean might compel the French to concentrate most of their ships in that sea. But a new scare in the winter of 1851–2 led to second thoughts in case the French were able to make a surprise move with their steamers from Toulon to the English Channel.[13] A Tory Board of Admiralty found itself grappling with the same problem in November 1852.

A month later, Aberdeen, as Prime Minister of a new coalition government, was also taking the French threat very seriously. In striking contrast to the trust which he had been willing to place in Louis-Philippe and Guizot in the mid-1840s, he now stressed the importance of co-operation with the eastern powers against France: 'If he [Napoleon III] thinks us divided, he will fall on us ... We should begin by being beaten even with equal numbers. Fifty thousand Frenchmen would beat fifty thousand Englishmen; and we have not so much to oppose a sudden invasion.'[14] Towards the end of 1853, even when the Admiralty was preparing for a possible war with Russia, French naval activities were still being closely scrutinised. It was ironic that the British navy, which had been so much strengthened since the mid-1840s, was about to find itself allied with the power it had been primarily designed to fight.

The Crimean War

Among the wars caused by failures in diplomacy and statecraft, the Crimea must rank high. Nicholas I, as we have seen, believed that he had secured an understanding of sorts with the British government in 1844. But the events of 1849 – when Britain stood by Turkey against Austrian and Russian demands for the surrender of Hungarian rebels – should have given him some insight into the nature of British politics. Admittedly Palmerston was then in the Foreign Office, while liberals and radicals were in a state of great excitement as the autocrats successfully counter-attacked against the revolutionaries of 1848. From December 1852, however, Aberdeen was Prime Minister of a coalition ministry, with Palmerston relegated to the Home Office. The Tsar, increasingly fearful that the Ottoman Empire might soon collapse, and troubled in any case by Austrian and French activity in the Near East, too readily assumed that this was a ministry with which he could do business.

Lord John Russell as Foreign Secretary, responded to the Tsar's overture on 9 February 1853. He discounted the danger of an imminent crisis, and urged restraint and reliance on the 'mutual concert between the Great Powers'. But he was perhaps too civil as well as too verbose. He referred to the 'exceptional protection' afforded to the Sultan's Christian subjects by the Tsar which, though 'burthensome and inconvenient, . . . [was] no doubt prescribed by duty and sanctioned by Treaty'.[15] But pleasantries which were intended to calm may have had the opposite effect on Nicholas – especially when he could hardly have failed to notice the current strains in Anglo-French relations as the British succumbed to another invasion panic. The Tsar was tempted to think the time ripe to bid for more Russian influence over the Christian subjects of the Porte.

Consideration was already being given to Russia's military options in the event of a rupture with Turkey or an aggressive move by France. But the Tsar remained strangely blind to the effect that even diplomatic pressure on the Turks might have on his relations with Britain – and probably with Austria as well. In any case, neither his demands nor the tone in which they were made were such as the Turks could accept. Once committed to a forward policy, however, it was not easy for Nicholas to pull back without loss of face.[16]

There is no need to retell the sad and complicated story of the origins of the Crimean War. The very different reactions and perceptions of Aberdeen and Palmerston are, however, revealing and relevant. The Prime Minister was temperamentally poles apart from his Home Secretary. Yet he was no pacifist, and there were occasions when he was ready to adopt a tough stance in foreign affairs. In Europe, his great aim was international stability. He also wished to avoid situations which might strengthen revolutionary or subversive forces. In this respect he and a number of other leading figures regarded Russia as, by and large, more trustworthy than France under Napoleon III. Furthermore, Aberdeen was no friend to the Muslim Turk.

Palmerston, in contrast, thought this an occasion for blunt speaking to the Russians. He favoured the survival of the Ottoman Empire, contending that its existence served British interests better than any likely successor or successors. As in the later 1830s, he argued that Russia would back down if firmly opposed. In so far as he feared for the stability of Europe, he still preferred to be free to pick and choose between the powers. He favoured a pragmatic line against Aberdeen's conservative leanings. If there was a great power which he particularly feared, it was France, not Russia.[17]

Aberdeen's own efforts in 1853 to find a peaceful solution were further hampered by divisions within the cabinet, and – as the crisis developed – by a great upsurge of Russophobia among progressive opinion. Liberals and radicals (with the events of 1848–9 still fresh in their minds) became excited by the prospect of a triumph of some sort against autocracy. Aberdeen's intentions were also obstructed by the actions of other players (including the Turks). In the end, too, he was perhaps not sufficiently formidable or ruthless a politician to make full use of such opportunities as presented themselves to realise his own objectives.

Consequently, British diplomacy was hesitant and ambiguous, while the presence (from June) of the Mediterranean fleet in Besika Bay at the mouth of the Straits was more than outweighed by the Russian occupation of the Principalities (modern Romania). This last step, however, brought the Austrians into play, and for a time in the summer of 1853 it seemed that all sides might have sufficient incentive to reach a diplomatic solution. This possibility was wrecked first by the Turks and later by the Russians. Then in October a Turkish ultimatum led to the outbreak of hostilities in the Balkans and the Caucasus. British and French warships were ordered through the Straits at the end of the month, but bad weather demonstrated the limitations of even steam-assisted battleships, the fastest ship taking all of nine days to complete the passage.[18]

A naval presence even at Constantinople was of no more than limited value. Nor was the potential of the fleets fully exploited. Ideally the allies should have moved on to deny Russian warships access to the southern Black Sea, while at the same time showing St Petersburg that they were doing their best to restrain the Turks. Given success in these two areas, another period of equipoise might have given the diplomats time to talk to some purpose. As it was, a Russian naval force seized an opportunity on 27 November to defeat a Turkish squadron at Sinope on the south shore of the Black Sea. This was a precipitate rather than an illegitimate act of war, but it was popularly described in Britain as 'a massacre'. Positions hardened, and in the new year the British and French fleets were instructed to neutralise the whole of the Black Sea. This time the allies had done more than was navally necessary. Their action deeply antagonised the Russians, who rejected all demands that they leave the Principalities. The resources of diplomacy were finally exhausted, and Britain and France declared war on 28 March 1854.

There was a final twist to this unhappy story. The Russians pulled out of the Principalities in the early summer of 1854. The decisive factor was the growing Austrian military threat on their western flank. With the advantage of hindsight it is tempting to believe that war might have been prevented if only the British, French and Austrians could have produced the proper mix of diplomacy and military pressure at the right time.

Not surprisingly, historians have continued to debate the causes of this conflict, and what British interests were really at stake as the crisis developed. While it might seem logical to emphasise the security of the British Mediterranean route to the East, there was as yet no Suez canal (not opened until 1869 and not fully used by the British until the 1880s). Even in the later Near Eastern crisis of 1877–8 (when the Russians did indeed almost reach the gates of Constantinople), some ministers thought it sufficient for Britain to hold Egypt.

Aberdeen's own objectives, once he had reconciled himself to war, were to free the Ottoman Empire from Russian influence and to strengthen it broadly within its current limits – presumably as a contribution to the overall balance of power. Clarendon went rather further, agreeing that the war had started in defence of Turkey, but vaguely suggesting that it had become enlarged to include 'European grounds', a review of all former treaties, and the establishment of a 'state of things which will render peace durable'. This guarded assessment might reflect the influence of inflamed 'liberal' opinion at home as well as of international considerations. Some of Palmerston's comments might be similarly interpreted, reference having been made already to his efforts to cultivate progressive opinion in Britain since the late 1840s. But in the case of the Crimean War, some evidence would seem to point to a desire to exploit the popular fervour to serve his ambitious foreign objectives rather than vice versa.

He touched, for instance, on grandiose schemes to cripple Russia as a great power. In March 1854 he outlined what he called his *'beau ideal'*. With sufficient allies he hoped to see Finland and the Aland

Islands transferred to Sweden, Poland re-established as an independent state, Turkey regain the mouth of the Danube, and Russia deprived of the Crimea, Circassia, Georgia and its Black Sea fleet. He talked of Russia being confronted by a stronger Turkey, Austria and Prussia. This had a Napoleonic rather than a British or primarily 'liberal' ring to it. He appeared to assume that the necessary coalition would not only take shape, but that its members would readily accept his new map of Europe. He seemed to discount or ignore the rivalry and suspicion which complicated Austro-Prussian relations, while acknowledging that their co-operation would be indispensable. At the same time it is not at all clear how he thought French interests and aspirations could be handled – given that France would be the most important single ally in the enterprise. In general it is difficult to reconcile this *beau ideal* with his own long-term respect for and distrust of France (a country whose potential had recently caused him to handle it with such discrimination). Although parts of his scheme would have delighted progressives in Britain, gains for France, Prussia and Austria would have been less welcome.[19]

Palmerston's ideas also clearly departed from widely held principles of British foreign policy, namely the desirability of evolutionary and orderly change, plus the assurance that the great-power balance would leave Britain well placed to manoeuvre this way and that to her own advantage. Aberdeen, not surprisingly and very sensibly, dismissed the *beau ideal* as a fantasy – a view it seems that was shared by most other ministers. Nevertheless, the Queen and Prince Consort continued for some time to fear that Palmerston and Napoleon between them were determined to overthrow much of the Vienna Settlement.[20]

Once war became probable, ministers understandably assumed that armies would be required to remove the Russians from the Principalities and to safeguard allied sea communications into the Black Sea. These were the initial objectives of the British and French troops which were sent to the Near East in 1854. At the same time the Baltic was an obvious scene of operations for the larger part of the British battlefleet. Control of the Gulf of Finland would make possible an effective blockade of Russia in the north. But the First Lord of the Admiralty also warned against any foolhardy attacks on the 'stone walls' of Sweaborg and Cronstadt – the fleet should not undertake 'an impossible enterprise'.[21]

Almost as the Anglo-French armies arrived at Varna on the Black Sea coast, so the Russians began to pull back from the Principalities, fearful of the Austrians on their right flank. The latter were eager to push their own interests, but not by war. The Russians, meanwhile, were determined to hold on to what remained of their treaty advantages in the Ottoman Empire. With a neutral Austrian army between themselves and their enemies south of the Danube, they saw no need to make concessions.

Ministers in London, on the other hand, were determined to reduce Russian influence in the Ottoman Empire to a minimum. Having sent a great expedition to the Black Sea, they had to be seen to achieve something positive. Palmerston argued that Russia's retreat provided no security for the future. Furthermore, the troops had to be used while they were in their prime. Ministers, he added, would 'lose caste in the world' at home and abroad if they allowed the war to end with only a 'small result'. Thus the cabinet agreed on 28 June to strike against Sevastopol – the Crimean key to Russian naval power in the Black Sea.[22]

In the circumstances this reasoning had a certain *ex post facto* logic. It is true that even the speedy capture of Sevastopol offered no guarantee that the Russians would agree to new terms. Even without a base at Sevastopol, the Russians might have posed future threats by the overland routes to the Ottoman Empire – routes which could be defended only by Austrians and Turk at the start of a future war. But while one can concur with Andrew Lambert that the British never had 'an agreed strategy, merely a collection of shifting perceptions', it is difficult to see what else could have guided them (having got into this situation) as long as the Russians refused to make at least some concessions. Without either Austria or Prussia as an ally, ministers could only hope that (by force in the Baltic and Black Seas, and by means of the blockade) the Russians might bend under pressure. Alternatively, allied successes might persuade other states to intervene on their side. As matters stood, even with the support of France, Britain could not act towards Russia in the grand manner of Charles XII or Napoleon.

Ministerial information on the Crimea itself was sketchy at best and often inaccurate. Admittedly, an appearance of discretion was left to the commander on the spot, but – as one of his colleagues noted – while a Wellington would not have proceeded to the Crimea without better intelligence on the enemy, the actual commander,

Lord Raglan, would have risked removal by his own government had he not acted. Indeed, popular feeling in Britain might have done the same to the cabinet had it not been firm. As it happened, the start of the operation was not inauspicious. Troops were quickly transferred by sea from Varna to the Crimea. It is even possible that under bolder leadership the armies might have taken Sevastopol. Instead they settled down to a long siege.

Not surprisingly in these circumstances, Sweden, Prussia and Austria were not tempted to join the war. Only the Piedmontese, anxious to gain support for their ambitions in northern Italy, later sent a small force. Setbacks in the Crimea, with reports of maladministration and unnecessary suffering among the troops, speedily undermined the Aberdeen coalition. Palmerston became Prime Minister at the start of 1855, and he prosecuted the war with as much vigour as Britain's own resources and her allies would permit.

Basically it remained a war of attrition, though one fortunately which the Russians could ill afford despite the fact that so little of their territory was directly exposed to attack. Allied forces in the Crimea were soon being more regularly and easily supplied than the troops opposing them. Large Russian forces were also tied up in the defence of positions in the Baltic – notably around St Petersburg.[23] In due course economic warfare cut Russian exports by 80 per cent and imports by one-third. The general reduction in economic activity also meant reduced customs returns. Inflation added to the strains on the economy and increased the danger of instability within the empire.

Sevastopol was finally stormed in the autumn of 1855. The British hoped for further successes, but the French were much less enthusiastic. Peace became a possibility as the Russians reflected on their dismal prospects if the war continued – even if they suffered no major losses of territory. Palmerston, too, was reluctantly being obliged to revise his thinking. He now talked of creating 'a long line of circumvallation from the Baltic to Georgia and Circassia. In particular he hoped to weaken the Russians in the Baltic by a series of maritime assaults on such strong points as Cronstadt and even St Petersburg.[24] What might have been achieved by newly-developed inshore and amphibious forces (involving some 225 British ships) must, however, remain a matter for surmise.

But Palmerston's reluctance to contemplate an early peace may still seem surprising, especially given British suspicions of her ally,

France. Relations were expected to deteriorate with the latter after the war, and with this in mind the Admiralty continued to build steam-assisted ships-of-the-line and frigates. Even so economy-minded a First Lord as Sir James Graham defined British maritime superiority on 12 October 1855 as the ability to meet Russia, France and the United States 'on equal terms'. Eternal friendship with France was 'a vain delusion'.[25] Similarly, a crisis or conflict with the United States could not be ruled out.

The momentum towards peace increased early in 1856, though with Palmerston continuing to fight a delaying action. Doubtless some of this bluster was tactical to try to wring the maximum advantage from the peace talks. With other ministers he was also worried by the belligerent mood of much of the public. But there is reason to suppose that Clarendon, the Foreign Secretary, became increasingly influential. From his position at the heart of the talks in Paris he was in the best position to judge the mood of the other powers – the war-weariness of the French, the terms on which Austria was prepared to co-operate, and how far one could hope to push the Russians. The Treaty of Paris was signed on 30 March. Palmerston's letter to the Queen on the same day gives some insight into his mixed feelings:

> ... any great and important additional security against future aggressions by Russia could only have been obtained by severing from Russia large portions of its frontier territory, such as Finland, Poland and Georgia ... and to have continued the war long enough for these purposes would have required greater endurance than was possessed by your Majesty's Allies, and might possibly have exhausted the good-will of your Majesty's own subjects.[26]

Elsewhere in private he did not pretend that the peace was satisfactory: it was at best 'satisfactory for the present'.

Certainly the peace did no more than weaken the Russians temporarily. They were left with no fleet or naval base in the Black Sea, and they also lost southern Bessarabia and easy access to the Danube. They were required to give up their claims to certain rights of interference in Serbia and the Principalities and on behalf of the Christian subjects of the Sultan. The Turkish Empire was admitted to the European Concert and its independence was guaranteed by the Anglo-French-Austrian treaty of 15 April. Admittedly the damage inflicted on Russia had given the Turks a breathing space, but it remained to be seen what use they would make of it. Similarly, only time would reveal how the other signatories would react when Russians began to reassert themselves.

It was soon evident that the shock of defeat was leading to a number of determined Russian efforts to modernise the empire (thereby threatening to make it a more dangerous enemy in the future). Commitment to the defence of the conservative cause in Europe was replaced by the determination to win back what had been lost in 1854–6. The Russians had also been painfully aware of their inability during the Crimean War to find vulnerable British points at which to strike. Thus accelerated imperial expansion into Central Asia seemed desirable to add to British fears for the security of India.

Within Britain herself some effort was made to reform and modernise the nation's armed forces. The efficacy of the navy's 'great armament' was never tested in the Baltic, while after 1856 it was the French (not the British) who first built a large armoured warship. Nevertheless, during the war itself the Royal Navy had played the senior part in securing command of the Baltic and Black Seas, and in providing for the safe passage of the allied armies to the Crimea. But whereas the navy had generally outperformed the French, the British army had been increasingly overshadowed by its partner in the Crimea.[27]

Lord Panmure, shortly after his appointment as Secretary of State for War, offered an interesting analysis of the army's failings (see Document 12). Perhaps some of his complaints were excessive, but the weaknesses in command and control were obvious. More and better staff officers were imperative. Panmure himself implied that Britain could no longer rely on the chance emergence of a genius such as a Marlborough or a Wellington. He concluded (and here one suspects the influence of Palmerston) that Britain had to show herself able to fight a modern war if she was to persuade other leading countries to take her seriously at all times.[28]

A start to reform had been made in June 1854 with the separation of the oddly associated colonial and war departments. Palmerston further strengthened the powers of the new Secretary of State for War in 1855. But Graham in 1860 still thought the minister's authority, 'tho' large', was 'practically much hampered'. Above all the commander-in-chief's relationship with the minister was inadequately defined – a problem which persisted until after the Boer

War. Michael Partridge concludes that, while progress had been made, it was doubtful whether the revised machinery 'could have withstood the strains of a major military effort'.[29]

The British had overcome the worst supply problems to the Crimea by the spring of 1855, but they found it difficult to raise enough troops. A small French superiority in 1854 had at times developed into an advantage of three to one. Briefly there was even talk, but only talk, of some form of compulsory service. Clarendon was not alone in his opinion that 'in the eyes of foreign nations . . . our prestige has greatly diminished', especially when the French were primarily responsible for the taking of Sevastopol. Yet whatever damage the Crimea had done to Britain's reputation, the drive for radical and comprehensive reform soon lost momentum – and especially any idea of maintaining an army properly equipped for operations against a European foe. In short, in so far as the British aspired to be a continental European power, they were unprepared to pay the cost. The implications for British foreign policy were soon underlined by Bismarck and others.

Notes

1 Yapp, *Strategies*, pp. 272, 279.

2 Bourne, *Foreign Policy*, pp. 37–42, and *Palmerston*, pp. 579 ff. For the geographical, political and economic constraints on the Black Sea fleet see Daly, *Russian Sea Power*, chapters 4 and 5.

3 Bartlett, *Sea Power*, pp. 128–44.

4 Yapp, *Strategies*, pp. 295–6, 416–17.

5 *Ibid.*, pp. 272–96, 414–17.

6 Chamberlain, *Aberdeen*, pp. 303–5, 379–81.

7 This section is based in the main on Bartlett, *Sea Power*, chapter 4, and Partridge, *Military Planning*. See also Andrew D. Lambert, *Battleships in Transition: the creation of the steam battlefleet, 1815–60*, London, 1984.

8 Bartlett, *Sea Power*, pp. 190–2.

9 Gash, *Wellington*, pp. 242 ff. See also M. Partridge, 'The Russell cabinet and national defence, 1846–52', *History*, LXXIII, 1987, pp. 231–50.

10 Bartlett, *Sea Power*, pp. 155–74.

11 *Ibid.*, p. 174.

12 *Ibid.*, pp. 255, 271, 274.

13 *Ibid.*, pp. 186–7, 271, 273–4, 279.

14 H. W. V. Temperley and L. Penson, *Foundations of British Foreign Policy, 1792–1902*, Cambridge, 1938, p. 289.

15 Bourne, *Foreign Policy*, pp. 315–16.

16 A. Lambert, *The Crimean War: British grand strategy, 1853–56*, Manchester and New York, 1990, pp. 11–14. Note also the key studies by J. B. Conacher, *The Aberdeen Coalition, 1852–55*, Cambridge, 1968, and *Britain and the Crimea, 1855–56*, London, 1987.

17 Donald Southgate, *'The Most English Minister . . . ': the policies and politics of Palmerston*, London, 1966, p. 324.

18 Lambert, *Crimean War*, pp. 38–57.

19 Conacher, *Crimea*, pp. 139–40; J. Snyder, *Myths of Empire: domestic politics and international ambition*, Ithaca and London, 1991, pp. 158–65; E. D. Steele, *Palmerston and Liberalism, 1855–65*, Cambridge, 1991, pp. 46–7. Note that Steele argues that Palmerston tried to avoid war on a scale that would disrupt the economy.

20 Lambert, *Crimean War*, p. 86; Steele, *Palmerston*, p. 47.

21 Lambert, *Crimean War*, pp. 38–57, 86–7. For the Baltic see C. I. Hamilton, 'Sir James Graham, the Baltic campaign and war-planning at the Admiralty in 1854', *Historical Journal*, XIX, 1976, p. 91.

22 Lambert, *Crimean War*, pp. xvi ff.; Chamberlain, *Aberdeen*, pp. 94–6.

23 See, e.g., B. Greenhill and A. Giffard, *The British Assault on Finland 1854–55*, London, 1988.

24 Lambert, *Crimean War*, pp. 78, 293, 298–306.

25 *Ibid.*, pp. 310–11.

26 A. C. Benson (ed.), *The Letters of Queen Victoria, 1837–61*, London, 1907, iii. 232–3.

27 Hamilton, 'Graham', especially pp. 103–12, examines the reasons for the British delays. His forthcoming major study of Anglo-French naval rivalry between 1840 and 1870 will further illumine the limitations of the British navy and its leaders.

28 Sir George Douglas (ed.), *The Panmure Papers*, London, 1908, i. 46–50.

29 Partridge, *Military Planning*, pp. 59–60.

3

More diplomacy, less defence
1856–75

Crises with the United States

Economic warfare had been a major instrument in the struggle against Russia. But the British had found it prudent to employ it more selectively than in the past. Interference with neutral shipping in the great wars before 1815 had depended upon the brute power of the navy. It had been much resented by other maritime states. Use of this weapon had also been a major cause of the War of 1812 with the United States. By 1854 the British had reason to act more cautiously. They had no wish to provoke the Americans a second time – relations were delicate as it was. They had also to take account of the views of their ally, France.[1]

The Anglo-French declaration of March 1854 therefore renounced the use of privateers and promised (somewhat vaguely) that only 'effective' blockades would be considered legal. Harsher measures, however, might have been employed had the conflict persisted beyond the beginning of 1856. British conduct continued to be based firmly on diplomatic criteria and 'prudential considerations'. As it was, the war itself gave rise to some unduly optimistic expectations concerning the future efficacy of close blockade and inshore operations. The usefulness of – and the promise shown by – small steam-armoured gunboats stimulated interest in more aggressive inshore use of the navy. C. I. Hamilton comments that to many 'it appeared that technology had brought a new order of priority to naval warfare'.[2] The methods used by the British in the great age of sail might no longer be so appropriate.

C

The same scholar goes on to show that the Crimean War was not, in fact, an illuminating guide to the future. With adequate rail links to the Crimea the Russians might have frustrated the allied attack on Sevastopol. Russia also lacked the means to increase trade with Prussia to compensate at least in part for the interruption to sea-borne traffic. Contemporaries, however, took more account of the results than of their causes – or of the changes that might occur in the future.

It was therefore agreed in Paris in April 1856 that privateering should be abolished, while for a blockade to be binding (*obligatoire*) it had to be 'effective'. Other concessions were made to neutrals. The British again assented for reasons of diplomatic expediency and in the expectation that the overall gains might outweigh the losses. In private, Palmerston made important reservations. All was not settled in perpetuity. The Paris declaration had only the force of a treaty, and treaties could be abrogated. In any case there were various loopholes which could be exploited, and in practice it would be possible to stretch the definition of contraband of war. The restraints would be 'hardly crippling'. Palmerston was particularly anxious to retain the means to paralyse the commerce of the United States at sea in any quarrel with that country. This was one of the few vulnerable points of the Americans.

During the Crimean War the British had had further reminders that war was still possible with the United States, especially when they themselves were deeply engaged elsewhere. Although the Webster–Ashburton treaty of 1842, the Oregon settlement of 1846 and the Clayton–Bulwer treaty of 1850 had eased tensions over the Canadian frontier and the management of any canal linking the Caribbean with the Pacific, the British still feared American ambitions in Cuba, Central America and even Canada. Their hopes that the Anglo-French alliance (from 1854) might act as a restraint on the United States were short-lived. As relations deteriorated with France, so the British had to look to their own ingenuity and resources to protect their interests in the New World.[3]

In any case, it was not long after the ending of the Crimean War that Palmerston himself reluctantly admitted that few in Britain shared his itch for a showdown with the United States. There was wide business and political agreement that Britain was now too dependent on America cotton and grain for a breach to be risked – except on the gravest of issues. *The Times* and *The Economist* argued that war with America would be the 'greatest of human calamities'. It was increasingly believed that Britain could not resist American expansion in Central America. Trade might even profit from American intervention in a region noted for its anarchy, lethargy and general backwardness.

Meanwhile, relations with the United States had to be seen in a broader context. In December 1856 Clarendon remarked that Britain might ultimately find herself involved in a simultaneous crisis or conflict with Russia, France and the United States. He personally believed that Britain could hope for success against the United States only with French support. Some admirals in 1858 not surprisingly re-opened the case for a three-power naval standard, with R. S. Dundas demanding a squadron in North American waters 'sufficient to command respect' from the United States which might otherwise be tempted to exploit an Anglo-French war. Others, including the Queen and Lord Derby, were even more fearful of a long- term threat from Russia. On 1 January 1859 Edmund Hammond, the leading official in the Foreign Office, warned of a future struggle 'with Russia for naval supremacy [in the Far East], and, at all events, for political influence in China and Japan'.[4]

Such gloomy prognostications encouraged politicians and diplomats to see what could be done to reduce Anglo-American friction. New agreements were concluded in 1860 relating to Central America. Admittedly this still left some unresolved issues. The opening up of Japan by Commodore Perry from 1853 was only one example of just how far American ambitions were beginning to stretch. Seward, who became Secretary of State in 1861, seemed determined to establish the United States on at least the lower rungs of the great-power ladder. The leading question of the hour for Americans, however, was the fate of the Union. Both North and South were preparing for war. But the British, for their part, not unreasonably feared that arms collected for one conflict might be put to other uses – exactly as Seward himself hoped.

An effective defence for British North America, however, proved as elusive as ever. As Lord Stanley had noted in 1844, 'though much has been said . . . little or nothing has been done' on this subject. The latest plans, driven by the desire to economise on imperial defence as a whole, envisaged the concentration of troops at just a few key points in British North America. These footholds would be hastily reinforced in the event of an emergency. It would be left to the navy to inflict what damage it could on American shipping and coastal towns from bases in Halifax and Bermuda. In 1861 relations were sufficiently tense for more troops to be hurried across the Atlantic.

Ministers nevertheless wondered whether such preparations were more likely to deter or provoke a people whose mood was unpredictable and whose language was felt to be so full of brag and bluster that the orators themselves might not really know their own minds. Worse, if the Americans talked themselves into an unintended war, this would be less damaging to them than it would be to the British. Ultimately the Americans, if they were sufficiently determined, would prevail in Canada through sheer weight of numbers. Even the British navy in 1861 was hard pressed to find ships to serve in American waters, given renewed fears of France and its many commitments elsewhere in the world. At least the loss of Canada, though serious, would not be a fatal blow to Britain as a world power.

The outbreak of the Civil War brought mixed reactions in Britain. Palmerston would have welcomed a permanent break-up of the Union (with a 'prosperous monarchy' in Mexico as a further obstacle to American ambition). But he and his supporters were always aware that war in support of a slave state would never be countenanced by powerful groups in Britain. Canada still seemed vulnerable, whatever the strain imposed on the North by the Civil War. The admirals were less confident than Palmerston that the navy could demolish the coastal towns of the United States, and were more fearful of the damage that might be suffered by British shipping.

War was narrowly averted in the winter of 1861–2 when a Northern warship intercepted a British ship, the *Trent*, and removed two Confederate agents. There were other problems during the war, but in the end the catastrophe of direct British involvement was avoided (according to Kenneth Bourne) by the 'collective wisdom of the Cabinet . . . rather than by the consistent good sense of any individual member'. Although the South was recognised as a belligerent, it was not acknowledged as an independent state. Nor did the British challenge the North's naval blockade of the South. It is true that as the North moved towards victory, so Palmerston still hoped to impress 'the Yankees' with evidence of Anglo-French friendship.[5] But French attention was being diverted from Mexico by the rise of Bismarckian Prussia, and Palmerston thereby lost his last hope of an improvement in the balance of North America to Britain's advantage. The victorious North was soon demanding redress for certain British actions during the Civil War – and particularly for Northern shipping losses at the hands of the British-built Confederate commerce raider, the *Alabama*.

New defence problems, 1856–65

There were several major extra-European calls upon the army after the Crimean War. In addition to Canada, provision had to be made for the Indian Mutiny (1857) and the Second China War (1856–60). But the fact that these occurred, and were (in due course) handled with relative success, worked in conjunction with powerful vested interests to discourage radical army reform on the lines envisaged by Lord Panmure's memorandum of 1855. Home and imperial defence, not the capacity to fight on the Continent against a European foe, continued to determine the army's character and composition. Nor did the British develop an interest in elaborate staff planning. The new Camberley Staff College of 1858 represented only a modest advance. Inquiries into military administration brought limited additions to the changes effected by Palmerston in 1855. Michael Partridge concludes that there existed only 'an erratically functioning bureaucratic machine', subject to constant changes dependent on political circumstances and the current balance of power among the various authorities who shared responsibility for national defence.[6]

Military preparation and thinking continued to diverge from continental models. Imperial needs required long-service volunteer troops, not short-service conscripts. Palmerston himself agreed that Britain could not copy the conscript armies of the continental powers. The structure of the national economy and society dictated that defence rested upon command of the seas. He was also convinced that Britain's strength need not be measured merely by what could be immediately deployed: the knowledge that she could act to great effect in a crisis could 'often powerfully influence the course of events'. On the other hand, Palmerston himself conceded in the Commons in 1858 that Russia and France, as well as the United States, were 'so far independent of naval warfare that even a naval reverse does not materially affect them'.[7] This was a remarkable admission.

The European wars between 1859 and 1871 were of such brief duration that they provided little up-to-date evidence of what navies might achieve. But each conflict emphatically underlined the disparity between the British army and those of the continental powers. Britain's problems were also intensified by the fact that after 1856 the Russian government no longer held Napoleon III at arm's length. Its determination to revise the Treaty of Paris took precedence over its old ideological prejudices. Indeed, Russia was now trying to trim and balance between the powers in the fashion of the British between 1815 and 1853 – and with the British usually cast as the enemy.

Palmerston, having helped to create this state of affairs, at least recognised the importance of good relations wherever and whenever possible with France. Given that Britain had to be absolutely secure at sea, he was ready – without 'complacency or weakness' – to cultivate French amity.[8] But for this display of common sense he was again made to suffer at the hands of his domestic political opponents. A heterogeneous coalition brought down his government when he tried to amend the law of conspiracy in 1858 following an attempt on the life of Napoleon III.

Palmerston returned to office in 1859 in the midst of a new invasion panic and with national feeling running even more strongly against France. Sympathy for the Italian cause did not reduce British suspicion of Napoleon III when he became involved in a war with Austria over the future of northern Italy. But Palmerston himself was to the fore among those in the cabinet who tried to balance defence preparedness with selective conciliation of France. The two governments were even able to negotiate a commercial treaty despite the tension, and occasionally contrived to work together over Italian questions. The British once again found that through co-operation they could sometimes lay a restraining hand on the French.

Nevertheless the latest defence panic was of real importance, and it produced large-scale action both to strengthen the navy and to improve the land defences of the British Isles (1858–61). The completion in 1858 of a large and well-defended French naval base at Cherbourg in the English Channel found the British counterpart at Portland (begun ten years earlier) less than half complete. The alarm deepened when it was reported early in 1859 that in the larger classes of steam warships there was little to choose between the British and French fleets. Indeed, on some counts it was possible the French were ahead. The French were also the first to build a large sea-going ironclad, *La Gloire*. The Admiralty responded quickly – thanks to British financial and industrial power – with the more powerful *Warrior*. She had an iron hull as well as armour. But impressive as she was, she stood at the beginning (not the peak) of an era of experimentation in British ship design. Several years elapsed before the Admiralty felt satisfied with its lead in ironclads. The British were much assisted in the later 1860s as their rival became preoccupied with developments in Germany.

The scare of 1856–61 had had much wider effects upon defence thinking. Early in 1859 the First Lord of the Admiralty warned Parliament that the navy was not 'in a proper and adequate state' for the defence of the British Isles. This was followed later in the year by a warning from a Royal Commission on the defence of the United Kingdom that it was no longer possible to look to the navy alone for security. Palmerston took up its recommendation that the major dockyards should be fortified at a cost of £11 million. Additions were made to the auxiliary forces for home defence. Between 1859 and 1865 the defence estimates rose by one-fifth to nearly £26 million.

The early 1860s witnessed the climax of nearly twenty years of effort to find a defence against either invasion or major attacks on key centres such as the dockyards. If the navy could not guarantee security, and if sufficient regular troops could not be provided, more reliance had to be placed – so the reasoning went – on fortifications and volunteer auxiliary forces. For a time the Treasury and Gladstone had little choice but to fund these new armaments, but the sense of urgency fell away after a few years. Work on the dockyard forts was not completed until 1880, by which time some were already becoming obsolete. Of the approaches to London, only the Thames was defended. Ireland remained exposed. As for the volunteer movement, the early surge of enthusiasm was not maintained. Only a few units were ever classed as of having significant military value. Palmerston himself thought the volunteers would be revealed as 'a shopkeeper force' if subjected to close scrutiny. Fortunately, as Michael Partridge notes, by 1870 defence planners were beginning to return to the traditional faith in the navy – provided it could be speedily mobilised. There was a greater appreciation of the fact the while small raids might achieve surprise, a serious invasion attempt could not. It was also acknowledged once again that if the navy could not save the nation from invasion, it could not save it from starvation and economic ruin.[9]

At this time much uncertainty still surrounded the design of capital ships. During the 1860s it was not a new battlefleet, but a miscellany of ironclads which took to the water. It is true that the Admiralty was ill equipped to preside over a period of techno-logical innovation with all its implications for ships and naval warfare. But the difficulties and imponderables surrounding the design of major warships would have tested the best brains and institutions. Despite improvements in engines, sail was still essen-tial for a navy which had to operate over great distances. It was necessary to reconcile the competing demands of engines, coal bunkers, crew, sail, big guns and armour all within one ship. The underwater threat posed by the new self-propelled torpedo seemed so serious that some began to question if large ships had a future. Design thus became a matter of continual experiment, with the basic silhouette (especially of the biggest ships) changing as rapidly as the feminine fashions of the day. The naval engagements of the time hardly clarified the situation. The biggest action, that at Lissa, was most memorable for the sinking of the Italian flagship by ramming. Only the American Civil War lasted long enough for economic warfare to make an impact.[10]

The victorious North ended this conflict with a large if miscel-laneous fleet. This was big enough for it to be closely monitored by the British for some years thereafter. The latter were quick to build superior ships when the Americans introduced a fast new cruiser. Such raiders also occasioned interest in the improvement and better security of key imperial bases. Obviously a large and scattered empire had too many vulnerable points for effective local protec-tion to be provided everywhere. In 1867 Captain J. C. R. Colomb (RN) supplied an important analysis of Britain's defence problems in his book, *The Protection of our Commerce and Distribution of our Naval Forces Considered*. He argued that Britain, the empire and the network of sea communications formed a single whole. The navy provided the shield through its command of the sea; the army was the spearhead for attack, to be deployed wherever it was needed. Only India required a large permanent garrison.

In the late 1860s both service departments were interested in mobile reserves – the navy with its 'flying squadron', and the army in the creation of an effective reserve of troops at home to be sent (under naval protection if required) to any region under threat. Both were necessary, as Liberals and Tories alike looked for cuts in the service estimates, and tried to reduce the numbers of ships and troops scattered around the empire. India and Canada remained in a different category. Both might be threatened by large modern armies. The British were particularly determined to hold India, and could draw some comfort from Russia's logistic problems in Asia, and the possibility that she might prove vulnerable to counter-attack in the Black Sea. But Canada seemed ultimately doomed in the event of a determined American assault.

Palmerston and the limits of British power

Palmerston in his day was accused of many faults – or worse – in his conduct of foreign affairs, and where the mid-Victorian critics led many historians have followed. Thus he stood – and stands – charged with bullying weak states, with meddling unnecessarily in the affairs of others, and with generally being too assertive and interventionist in his dealings with great and small states alike. One consequence of his policy was heavier defence spending. This was needed either to handle the crises he had caused, or to protect Britain from the resentment he had provoked. Lord Granville, soon after becoming Foreign Secretary in 1870, complained that Palmerston had 'wasted the strength derived by England from the great war by his brag'.

Reference has already been made to Palmerston's frustrated belligerence in his dealings with the United States, to the controversies surrounding as well as the success of his policies in the crisis with France over the Near East in 1840, and above all to his role in the Crimean War, which might have resulted in a much greater conflict had he had his way. That he practised 'gunboat diplomacy' (which could extend to the use of troops, as in the two China wars) against weak states and peoples is not in dispute. He himself claimed that there existed 'half-civilised governments ... [which required] a dressing every eight or ten years to keep them in order'. They needed to feel as well as see the stick. Even with the bigger powers he was quick to 'show the flag', and often ostentatiously manoeuvred squadrons (preferably larger than their rivals) as a reminder that it was natural for 'the Police Man' to check what was going on. 'Diplomats and protocols,' he once remarked, 'are very good things, but there are no better peace-keepers than well-appointed three-deckers.'

Yet 'Palmerstonian' foreign policy was not a simple matter of belligerence, bullying and bluster. If his faith in gunboat diplomacy when dealing with refractory weaker peoples remained unshaken, he displayed a little more faith in his last years in their ability to learn how to live in accord with western notions of international intercourse. With respect to the great powers, instances have already been noted in this text of his readiness to try negotiation and conciliation even in defiance of the prejudices of many of his countrymen – notably after Louis Napoleon had emerged as the key figure in France. As early as the Belgian and Spanish questions in the 1830s he had shown – in his own way – that he was alive to the possibility of restraining other powers by entangling policies of co-operation.

His experiences of the Crimean War also seemed to temper his thinking and conduct. Having failed to throw back Russia into the mid eighteenth century, and also having come to see how reluctant his countrymen were to quarrel with the United States, Palmerston took a more modest view of Britain's ability to assert herself internationally. Perhaps, too, the change was only to be expected of a man in his seventies. He conceded that the British people would not agree to the creation of something akin to a continental-type army. Even the world's biggest navy might be frustrated by a power which was prepared and able to sacrifice its seaborne trade and its coastal cities. From 1859 onwards his bold speeches often concealed not only uncertainties and divisions within his cabinet, but also doubts and reservations of his own. Overall he had become more cautious and calculating in the conduct of policy than the older interpretations would have us believe. Tensions with France from 1859 into the early 1860s were (as we have seen) handled with a particularly interesting mix of sensitive diplomacy and arms increases.

In the first great European episode after the Crimean War, the unification of Italy, British ministers appeared to achieve all that was necessary through diplomatic influence and the presence in 1860 of a naval squadron in the Straits of Messina. But in reality, cabinet divisions ensured that British foreign policy was often uncertain and erratic. Palmerston and Russell at times tried to

co-operate with Napoleon III – though more with an eye to restraining France than in order to help Italy. The key players were the
Austrians, Cavor, Napoleon III and Garibaldi – in what they did
not as well as what they did do. It was particularly fortunate for the
British that both France and Austria were sobered by the experience
of war in 1859 in the north of Italy. Even so, Palmerston followed
the ensuing events with considerable apprehension.

The fate of Italy was being left increasingly to the Italians themselves in 1860. The British were gradually reassured by Cavor's
efforts to avoid further great-power intervention, and to show his
independence of the French. This accorded with their own interests.
In June 1860 an attempt was made to persuade Garibaldi to content
himself with Sicily. Similarly, it was to sustain great-power non-
intervention that London declined a French proposal for a 'joint
naval blockade' to stop Garibaldi and his forces crossing from Sicily
to Naples. The resulting naval inaction meant, however, that the
crossing could go ahead. The collapse of Neapolitan resistance soon
followed, thus opening the way to the unification of most of Italy in
1860–1. Unification, once it came, was acceptable to the British. But
claims to moral leadership after the event misled contemporaries
into believing that the government was entitled to more credit than
it deserved.

The truth concerning the limits of British influence in Europe did
not become apparent until the Polish and Danish crises of 1863 and
1864. Public opinion compelled the government to express some
concern for the Poles at the start of their revolt against Russia.
Ministers duly tested the mood in St Petersburg, but backed off
once it became apparent that the Russians were in earnest. Unfor-
tunately Napoleon III, who had been more anxious to intervene, felt
that he had been let down by the British. Consequently Britain and
France were too much at odds to act in concert during the Danish–
German crisis over the future of Schleswig and Holstein. But
Palmerston in any case privately admitted in 1864 that war with
Prussia and Austria would be 'a serious undertaking'. While
Russell was airily talking of a British fleet at Copenhagen and a
French army on the Rhine, Palmerston was viewing the matter
from a broader perspective. He was particularly fearful of the
implications for the Low Countries if the French embarked upon
any major military enterprise. Meanwhile Bismarck, not surprisingly, was unimpressed by any British sympathy for the Danes – hence

his famous remark that if necessary her army could be arrested by a few Prussian policemen. In practice, the British would have found it difficult to send more than 20,000 troops.

Palmerston gave other evidence of his continued interest in the European balance of power and its relevance to Britain. He was much more impressed by Russian potential than he had been in the 1830s or 1850s. In 1865 he considered a strong Germanic state an essential component of the balance owing to his belief that Russia was destined to acquire an empire on the scale of the Romans. At the same time he continued to be impressed by the power of France (see Document 13).[11]

Muriel Chamberlain stresses the degree to which Palmerston's public rhetoric reinforced the lasting myth of British influence in Europe. Great discrimination, she adds, is needed to see just how much he did in fact achieve 'by skilful playing of the diplomatic game' in a world of five great powers.[12] Certainly he can be credited with some personal successes – notably in 1840 – a case where another minister might have acted very differently or to less effect. In this and in other instances one also notes his careful evaluation of the interests and intentions of the other powers. It was in 1854–6, above all, that he seemed most in danger of losing his sense of proportion. British influence in Europe thereafter was fairly modest, and Palmerston – in private – showed considerable awareness of the nation's limitations. His successors might have felt that they were pursuing more moderate courses. They also congratulated themselves on their cuts in defence spending. Yet in foreign, if not defence, policy Palmerston had been moving in a similar direction. As for the naval economies which were achieved by the 1870s, many of these were due to France's growing preoccupation with Bismarck's Germany.

Experiments in compromise

Even under Palmerston's successors there was no complete adoption of a policy of consistent non-intervention in Europe. Indeed, Paul Hayes describes British policy in the later nineteenth century as one of 'limited liability' in Europe 'which actually required British diplomacy to be rather active'.[13] Gladstone – for one – was anxious that Britain's voice should be heard and her interests protected. He was noted for his desire to promote international law and discourage the practice of *realpolitik*, but he was also moved by more down-to-earth considerations.

Britain had to take care not to promise more than she could deliver, and thereby lessen her standing in Europe in the way that she was felt to have done over the Danish duchies. Conservatives as well as Liberals were anxious to economise on defence at home and in the empire. Some strongly believed that Britain already had responsibilities enough in the world: that the advance of free trade, the promotion of international law and great-power restraint together constituted a promising way forward and one in accord with British interests. This was not merely a product of woolly-minded idealism. Recent events in Europe, the Indian Mutiny, and a number of other episodes could all be interpreted as warnings that the days of bold bluffs, politics and empire-building on the cheap (relatively speaking) were coming to an end. Sea power, too, was being challenged by new railway construction. There were even – for the most perceptive – early indications that Britain's industrial lead was not what it had been. Britain had good cause to proceed with care.

British respect for the military potential of the United States was by now well established. Gladstone argued that diplomacy must of necessity be the main instrument in future dealings with Washington. Clarendon in December 1865 had already declined a French suggestion that the two powers should co-operate to discourage American intervention in the Mexican civil war. The Tory ministries of 1866–8 were equally cautious, and lowered North America in Britain's list of strategic priorities. Cardwell, early in the Gladstone government of 1868, planned to cut colonial garrisons as a whole by almost half to some 26,000, of which only 3,000 were to be stationed in British North America. Even so, fears persisted that the United States might take the offensive if Britain were involved in a crisis in Europe. The First Lord in December 1870 listed both Russia and the United States as major influences on naval policy.[14]

The main point at issue between London and Washington was the British connection with the activities of the Confederate commerce raider, the *Alabama*, during the Civil War. Complicated negotiations finally resulted in the Treaty of Washington of 8 May 1871 whereby the American claims for damages from Britain were referred to arbitration. Kenneth Bourne sums up the thrust of

British policy towards the United States in the difficult years after 1865 in the following terms: '[There was] an explicit recognition that Great Britain could never again hope to challenge the will of the United States on the continent of North America. But this was realism, not friendship.'[15] Similarly, when faced by possible American intervention in Cuba in the early 1870s the British had no thought of lending support to Spain. Their main concern was to avoid a Spanish-American war. This could pose a serious threat to their extensive trading activities, especially with New Orleans.[16] Indeed, trade continued to be one of the most consistent forces making for easier Anglo-American relations. British adoption of free trade had boosted parts of the United States economy, and improved American access to Canadian markets. Although Americans continued to dream of expansion northwards, conquest had come to seem unnecessary. Indeed, the United States became so introspective that the British were taken by surprise in 1895 by its intervention in a frontier dispute affecting Venezuela and British Guiana. This crisis reminded the British that they could not afford to quarrel with the United States, and was soon followed by renewed disengagement from the New World.

During the Franco-Prussian War of 1870–1 Gladstone, in his own eyes, tried to steer between the extreme options of a 'Quixotic' or futile intervention and total inaction. Indeed, on 16 July, the day after the start of the war and fearful that Belgian neutrality might be infringed, he called on the War Office 'to study the means of sending 20,000 troops to Antwerp with as much promptitude as at the *Trent* affair we sent 10,000 to Canada'. But this, he later admitted, was 'a far outlook'. His Secretary of State for War had no wish to act, and insisted that even a modest plan would require an increase to the army: a sign that the British had still not created the effective mobile reserve which they talked about on paper.[17] Gladstone himself was briefly troubled by this weakness. In practice, the government found both France and Prussia were willing to respect Belgian neutrality, but clearly that state was protected by the self-restraint of the two belligerents in 1870–1 rather than by Britain.

The British had viewed Franco-Prussian rivalry from 1866 with mixed feelings. Unease over the rise of Bismarck and the Prussian army was tempered by distrust of Napoleon III. Until the German victory at Sedan, France was still regarded as the leading power in Europe. There was some swing of feeling towards the French in the winter of 1870–1 once the extent of Prussian success and ambition became apparent. Prussian politics and militarism had often caused unease, but the British were soon broadly persuaded that the new Germany was a satisfied power which might be expected to improve the balance on the Continent against both France and Russia. North German Protestantism also possessed great appeal for Gladstone at a time of Papal self-assertion.

Admittedly in 1874–5 there were passing fears that Bismarck might again be looking for an excuse to crush France. The concern shown by a new Tory government during the 'War-in-Sight' crisis of 1875 was prompted by more than Disraeli's itch to cut a dash among the powers. In 1874 there had been renewed European speculation that Bismarck might again be looking for ways to put pressure on France – either by an extension of the *Kulturkampf*, or by exploitation of a civil war in Spain. It was episodes such as these which prompted a variety of British diplomatic efforts to defuse the tension. But gone were the days (in the 1830s and 1840s) when Palmerston had wished to turn Spain into a client or ally. It was felt sufficient to encourage Spanish neutrality, political stability and economic liberalism. Even Britain's oldest ally, Portugal, felt a hint of reserve as the Foreign Office lowered its profile in Iberian politics as an example to the other powers.[18]

British diplomats similarly tried to prevent further European colonisation in North Africa. There were fears in 1875–8 that, if the latest Near Eastern crisis led to the breakup of the Ottoman Empire, the process would not stop there. This was one reason for Britain's refusal to consider Bismarck's suggestions that she occupy Egypt. Meanwhile Spanish and French interest in Morocco was carefully monitored.

In general the British had few worries at sea in the 1870s; the navies of the United States and France were in a state of decline, while the Russians were largely devoting their resources to other tasks. It is true that the Russians took advantage of the Franco-Prussian War in 1870 to repudiate the Black Sea clauses, and the Gladstone ministry was able to save only a little face by regularising the change at a conference in London in the winter of 1870–1. With that crisis out of the way, and with easier relations with the United States, naval retrenchment proceeded under Gladstone and Disraeli alike. By 1874 they had sharply reduced the numbers of warships deployed outside home waters, including the Mediterranean.

For the time being it seemed that Britain herself, her main lines of communication, and much of the empire could be protected with relative ease. Thus, the fleet in 1874 could confidently be rated as equal to the combined strength of its two nearest rivals. Unfortunately there was a price to pay. Complacency and lethargy easily set in – despite some warnings of danger. Not even the war scare with Russia in 1878 produced more than a temporary flurry of concern. By 1884–5, however, the challenges from France at sea and Russia on land (and later at sea) could no longer be ignored.[19]

Notes

1 This section draws heavily on C. I. Hamilton, 'Anglo-French sea-power and the Declaration of Paris', *International History Review*, IV, 1982, pp. 166–92.

2 *Ibid.*, p. 189.

3 For Britain and the American Civil War see Bourne, *North America*, pp. 180–201.

4 Bartlett, *Sea Power*, p. 276 and n.; Bourne and Watt, *Studies*, p. 191. See also Martin Papers, British Museum, London, Add MSS 41410, ff. 120–4; Gladstone Papers, Add MSS. 44589, ff. 4–5; and Benson, *Victoria*, iii. 417.

5 Bourne, *Foreign Policy*, p. 92, and *North America*, p. 255; Steele, *Palmerston*, p. 254.

6 Partridge, *Military Planning*, p. 64. See also Beckett and Gooch, *Politicians*, p. 19.

7 Steele, *Palmerston*, pp. 198, 293, 307.

8 *Ibid.*, p. 316. See also M. J. Salvouris, *'Riflemen Form': the war scare of 1859–60 in England*, New York and London, 1982.

9 Partridge, *Military Planning*, pp. 100–46.

10 C. I. Hamilton, 'The Royal Navy, *la Royale*, and the militarisation of naval warfare, 1840–70', *Journal of Strategic Studies*, VI, 1983, especially pp. 199–209.

11 Steele, *Palmerston*, p. 262. See pp. 291 and 316 for Palmerston's particular fear of Russia in 1865.

12 Muriel E. Chamberlain, *Lord Palmerston*, Cardiff, 1987, pp. 122–4. The degree to which Britain could exert influence through her navy is discussed at length by P. M. Kennedy, *The Rise and Fall of British Mastery*, New York, 1976, chapters 6–8, and more briefly by C. J. Bartlett, *Britain Pre-eminent*, London, 1969, chapter 8.

13 A. Ramm (ed.), *The Political Correspondence of Mr Gladstone and Lord Granville, 1868–76*, Camden 3rd series lxxxi, London, 1952, i. 139;

T. R. Gourvish (ed.), *Later Victorian Britain, 1867–1990*, Basingstoke, 1988, p. 154.

14 G. E. Buckle (ed.), *Letters of Queen Victoria*, London, 1926, 2nd series, i. 594. But note that earlier, when pressed by the Queen to uphold Britain's treaty commitments to Portugal and Belgium, Clarendon had pointed to the lack of public support (*ibid.*, i. 590). See also Bourne and Watt, *Studies*, p. 204.

15 Bourne, *Foreign Policy*, p. 96.

16 C. J. Bartlett, 'British reaction to the Cuban insurrection of 1868–78', *Hispanic American Historical Review*, XXXVII, 1957, pp. 299–301.

17 John Morley, *The Life of W. E. Gladstone*, London, 1903, ii. 339. The evolution of the army, including its recruiting problems and the diverse calls upon it, are fully discussed by E. M. Spiers, *The Late Victorian Army*, 1868–1902, Manchester, 1992.

18 C. J. Bartlett, 'The diplomatic relations of Britain and Spain, 1868–1880', *Bulletin of the Institute of Historical Research*, XXX, no. 81, 1957, pp. 118–19.

19 J. T. Sumida, *In Defence of Naval Supremacy, 1889–1914*, Boston and London, 1989, pp. 10–11.

4

From the Mediterranean
to the Far East
1875–1901

The Near Eastern question, 1875–8

In the last quarter of the nineteenth century it was the vast region stretching from the Mediterranean to the north-west frontier of India which gave British defence planners their biggest headaches. By the end of the 1890s the areas of concern had been further extended to parts of China and the neighbouring seas. The existence of what was usually seen as a satisfactory balance in Europe helped to concentrate attention upon the Ottoman Empire, Persia and Afghanistan, and (in due course) Egypt and the Nile Valley. Russia's Asiatic railway-building in particular seemed to present a major and perhaps insoluble threat to the approaches to India. Differences also developed with France once that country began to recover from the defeat of 1870–1. Thus the Admiralty from the late-1880s was haunted by the possibility of effective co-operation between the French and Russian navies – especially in the Mediterranean and at the Straits.

There had been hopes in some quarters until the early 1870s that the Russians might permit the emergence of an effective buffer zone between their Asiatic empire and that of Britain in India. The Gladstone government of 1868 in particular tried to pursue what sceptics characterised as the policy of 'masterly inactivity' – a policy designed to give the Russians no excuse to take the offensive themselves. Russian assurances, however, were belied by their own conduct. The advance into Central Asia continued. The conquest of Khiva in 1873 caused particular concern.

Worse was soon to follow with the re-opening of the Near East-ern Question in 1875–8. The trouble began with anti-Turkish risings in Bosnia-Herzegovina. The unrest spread, and in 1876 Turkish massacres of Bulgarians further inflamed the situation. There were fierce Liberal attacks on the policy and attitude of Disraeli's Conser-vative government. In fact the cabinet itself was divided, with some ministers sharing the sense of outrage against the Turks. Nor was there unanimity as to the importance of British interests in the Otto-man Empire and Near East, and how these could best be defended.

Disraeli himself made various tactical shifts during this period of crisis, but Richard Millman detects a basic consistency in his thinking. Above all, he argues, Disraeli was determined to en-hance British influence and prestige, and to put an end to the marginalisation of his country in European great-power politics. This was caused primarily by the current understanding among Russia, Germany and Austria-Hungary (the first Three Emperors' League or *Dreikaiserbund*). Disraeli probably exaggerated its solidity (it showed signs of strain in 1874–5 during spells of Franco-German tension). To enhance British influence he was prepared to consider a wide range of options, including deals with Russia at the expense of the Turks. Even a partition of the Ottoman Empire was con-ceivable in certain circumstances.[1] Disraeli was also anxious to avoid a recurrence of the events of 1853–4 in the Near East. He insisted on 19 October 1876, 'The vile Crimean war might have been prevented by firmness on our part.'[2] But Britain could exert little influence until 1878, partly because his colleagues (as well as opinion in Britain) was too divided, and because the other powers lacked sufficient incentives to co-operate with Britain.

The Prime Minister meanwhile busied himself as an amateur strategist. As early as the autumn of 1876 he claimed that if the Russians reached Constantinople they could also reach the mouth of the Nile: 'Constantinople is the key to India, and not Egypt and the Suez Canal.' It was this sort of remark which prompted one of his recent biographers to suggest that the British obsession with the Near Eastern Question was a product of 'ancient habit rather than clear thought'. British command of the eastern Mediterranean would not necessarily have been compromised by a Russian presence even at the Straits.[3] But the Prime Minister was on firmer ground on the subject of British freedom to use the Straits. In 1877 he was clearly anxious to see the Queen's forces engaged in offensive operations in the Black Sea if it came to a war with Russia. Here he was taking a line familiar to many strategists. With access to and command of the Black Sea the British could hope to put pressure on Russia in pursuit of a variety of objectives – including the defence of India.

From the start of the Russo-Turkish war in April 1877, Disraeli was determined – at the very least – to secure temporary British possession of Gallipoli to offset a Russian occupation of Constantinople. But cabinet divisions still permitted no more than modest preparations. Even a consensus on the importance of the Suez Canal did not lead to agreement as to how it should be defended. Some ministers thought control of Egypt and Crete sufficient to neutralise any threat from Russia at the Straits.

Ministers could at least agree to concentrate British warships in the eastern Mediterranean. The strengthening of garrisons in the region was begun in July 1877 – though only a modest force of 10,000 men was at first envisaged to be on hand in the event of an emergency in the Near East. The cabinet also refused to warn Russia that an occupation of Constantinople would be treated as a *casus belli*. Even the generals were divided over the desirability and feasibility of holding Gallipoli.[4] As it happened, delays in the Russian advance across the Balkans allowed ministers to persist in their inconclusive debate. Not until the winter of 1877–8 were Constantinople and the Straits coming under threat. Even then the British appeared so hesitant that when, in January 1878, they tried to open talks on possible co-operation with Austria-Hungary, they evoked only the most guarded of responses. Disraeli himself acknowledged that Britain did not possess the military force to defend Constantinople (a total of from 60,000 to 80,000 troops was thought necessary).

Nevertheless, by February 1878 the Russian advance was causing sufficient alarm among some ministers and sections of the public for Disraeli to be able to initiate some counter-measures. Parliament agreed to a supplementary defence vote of £6 million. The fleet was at last ordered through the Straits to the Sea of Marmora. Admittedly this was not entirely to the liking of the British admiral. What if Russian troops were to make a sudden move and occupy Constantinople or – worse – the Gallipoli shore of the Dardanelles (thereby threatening his line of communications with the Mediterranean)? Disraeli, in contrast, was buoyed up by the sanguine views of one of his military advisers.[5] Optimists and pessimists could at least approach a consensus on one point. Peace, it seemed, hung by a thread as the Russian and British governments each manoeuvred to impress the other with its resolve. As Millman remarks, any reasonable man would have given 'very long odds against a peaceful accommodation'. A British expeditionary force was being prepared, and some 7,000 native troops were ordered from India to Malta.

By the end of March, a greater sense of unity and purpose was developing within the cabinet. The Foreign Secretary, Lord Derby, had been primarily intent upon the avoidance of war. The divisions between him and the Prime Minister finally led to his resignation. His successor, Lord Salisbury, was in the interesting position of having recently been a critic of both Derby (ineffectual) and Disraeli (too extreme). But Russia's latest successes, and the harsh terms which she imposed on the Turks by the Treaty of San Stefano of 3 March 1878, persuaded him that Britain must take a stand. His fear of Russia at last outweighed his detestation of the Turks.

The more assertive mood in London was paralleled by growing reservations among the Russians. Awareness of the costs of the war was mounting in St Petersburg. Russian generals outside Constantinople felt increasingly uncomfortable at the prospect of renewed fighting with the Turks even if the latter were supported only by the British.[6] Finally, it was now the turn of the Russians to feel isolated as Vienna and Berlin reacted unsympathetically to the terms of San Stefano. Salisbury was thus well placed to launch a diplomatic offensive. His notable dispatch of 1 April 1878 (see Document 14) was constructive but firm. He spelt out Britain's interests in the future of the Straits, Suez and the Persian Gulf. It was impossible for her to accept the subordination of the Ottoman Empire to Russia.

St Petersburg did not admit defeat easily, but step by step the controversial Treaty of San Stefano was revised. Salisbury was much assisted by Peter Shuvalov, the very able and realistic Russian ambassador. The negotiations reached their climax at the Congress of Berlin in June 1878. The 'big Bulgaria' created at San Stefano (and widely seen as intended to serve as a Russian client and a stepping-stone to Constantinople and Gallipoli) was now split into three parts. The Turks regained control of all of the northern coast of the Aegean, thus adding to the security of the approach to the Dardanelles from the British point of view.

Salisbury also tried to improve the long-term prospects of the Turks in Asia. He did not believe that either Persia or Afghanistan constituted adequate barriers against further Russian advances towards the Gulf and India. A convention of 4 June guaranteed Asiatic Turkey against further Russian acquisitions. In addition, Salisbury attempted to safeguard British naval access to the Black Sea (whenever the 'independence of Turkey' was threatened or the Sultan did not appear to be a free agent). But as we shall see, the position at the Straits in the 1880s and 1890s was to be determined less by paper provisions than by the alignments and decisions of the other powers.

Disraeli claimed that he and his Foreign Secretary had secured 'peace with honour' in Berlin. Millman prefers to describe it as 'peace with prestige', fifteen years of 'self-effacement, embarrassment, and ignominy' having been dispelled at the Congress. Despite Disraeli's faults, he credits him with the greatest contribution of any individual to the return of Britain from the sidelines of European politics. Certainly, none of his leading colleagues had worked so single-mindedly in pursuit of that aim. The Near Eastern crises had supplied potent reminders that international influence had to be earned. In the end there was some substance to the claims of the famous 'jingoistic' music-hall song of the time. If the 'men' (in terms of soldiers) were hardly numerous, there could be no doubt of Britain's advantages in 'ships' and 'money'.

Yet in terms of British standing in Europe the achievement was short-lived. There were signs of slippage even before the formation of a new Liberal government in 1880. The errors of the latter were not the sole cause of Britain's growing international problems for much of the next decade. Bismarck by the end of 1879 (having concluded an alliance with Austria-Hungary) was anxious to to rebuild the *Dreikaiserbund* which had been the cause of so much frustration to Disraeli in 1875–7.

Egypt and Afghanistan

The effects of the Near eastern crisis of 1875–8 were not confined to the Balkans and Turkey in Asia. British suspicions of Russian activities in Central Asia increased, while ministers who might have been wary of resisting Russia at the Straits looked to Egypt as the key to Britain's shorter route to India.

Interest in an alternative to the Cape route to the East had developed long before the opening of the Suez Canal in 1869. Steamer services to Britain and India from either side of the isthmus of Suez were inaugurated in the 1830s. Aden was acquired in 1839, and the British set out to command both the Red Sea and the Persian Gulf. But if a canal at Suez might have seemed of obvious advantage to Britain, Palmerston from 1855 reasoned otherwise. He expected any such project to increase the influence of the French in Egypt. The canal had also to be seen in the context of the desire to make the Mediterranean 'a French lake'. He calculated that Britain was likely to lose any race to control the canal in an emergency. Her forces might in any case be engaged elsewhere when the French made their move, or there might be the usual shortage of troops ready for instant dispatch. Finally, a French army at Suez might be able to deny British troops in India passage to Alexandria.[7]

Tory and Liberal Ministries took much the same view until 1870. Cyprus and Crete were added to the list of British strategic interests in the Mediterranean. But completion of the canal in 1869 was followed a year later by the defeat of France at the hands of Germany. Gladstone argued in November 1870 that Britain had little to fear as long as the canal was not fortified. It would be a less aggressive measure to seize it during a war than in time of peace. As matters then stood, 'never was there less danger or likelihood of our being overpowered in the Mediterranean'.[8] This more temperate view prevailed throughout the 1870s. Disraeli's famous Suez Canal coup in 1875 did not preclude Anglo-French co-operation to handle an Egyptian financial crisis. Salisbury described the joint action as preferable either to a British monopoly (which would be 'very near the risk of war' with France), or to renunciation, which would leave 'France across our road to India'.

Again, when political turmoil gripped Egypt in the early 1880s, the Liberal government at first tried to co-operate with France. The British reluctantly occupied Egypt in 1882 and, having felt compelled to intervene, they continued to look for ways to disengage. But their efforts to 'internationalise' control (albeit with Britain as the chief 'mandatory' power) made no progress. Instead, they found themselves bearing the responsibility while other powers (notably France and Germany) drew benefits from their share in the management of Egyptian finances.

It took time before British ambivalence on the question of Egypt was gradually replaced by the conviction that it should be turned into one of the bastions of the empire. In the 1880s, with the improved efficiency of steamships, use of the canal increased at the expense of sail, which had to take the longer Cape route. Suez cut 5,600 miles off the voyage to India, and the passage from London could be completed in about twenty-four days by fast steamer. There was, however, a transition period while the British continued to give attention to the preservation of the Ottoman Empire and to the use or defence of the Straits.

Meanwhile, the defensive policy of the first Gladstone ministry with respect to the north-west frontier of India had become the object of increasing scrutiny by the Tories. As early as April 1875 Salisbury, as Secretary of State for India, expressed doubts as to whether Afghanistan could long survive as a neutral state. Disraeli feared that Russia would become the dominant influence in Kabul unless the Afghans were persuaded that Britain was the stronger of the two empires. The Near Eastern crisis from 1875 added to the sense of urgency. Skobelev, the Russian military governor in the Ferghana region, claimed in 1876–7 that even a small Russian force on the frontier 'would probably lead to a general uprising in India and the ruin of the British empire'.[9] In August 1878 a Russian military mission concluded a treaty of mutual support with the Afghan amir. In contrast a British mission which attempted to reach Kabul was turned back. The Second Afghan War followed.

The outcome was a military victory of sorts, but again at considerable cost to the economy of India. The Liberals on their return to office in 1880 were happy to reach an accommodation with a new amir. He proved to be an effective ruler and fortunately believed that he had more reason to fear the Russians than the British. The government was also given a Russian promise not to occupy Merv. But once again this was no more than a pause in the Great Game. Russo-Afghan territorial disputes persisted, and the Russians were soon pushing into regions to an extent which even a Liberal cabinet could not tolerate. Work was resumed on the strategic Quetta railway (suspended after the Second Afghan War). When the Russians went ahead and occupied Merv in February 1884, Herat, 'the main highway to India', was felt to be at risk. The secretary of state for India commented in 1884 that an 'attack on Herat will mean war with Russia everywhere'. When yet another border clash occurred – at Penj-deh in March 1885 – Gladstone and his colleagues decided that they had no option but to make a firm stand. Even so there were some critics. W. E. Baxter dashed off a pamphlet, *England and Russia in Asia*, protesting that his countrymen always seemed in need of an enemy. India was best defended by low taxes on its peoples and not by war in remote wastes. Was this not a case for arbitration?

The government, however, easily secured an £11 million vote of credit in April, the largest (apart from the Crimean War) since 1815. In India 25,000 troops were prepared for dispatch to Quetta. But the Liberals were divided on issues at home, and a political crisis in June brought Salisbury back into power at the head of a minority Conservative government. He promptly tried to end Britain's isolation among the powers. His effort to lure Germany away from Russia failed, but it was a sensible first step. Had it succeeded it might have lifted the *Dreikaiserbund*'s veto on the opening of the Straits and allowed British forces to threaten Russia in the Black Sea. Fortunately the Russians in September 1885 decided to give new assurances to Britain and surrendered their claim to the important Zulficar Pass. Some of them, including Skobelev, were also becoming more aware of the obstacles to an advance deep into Afghanistan.

The seach for security against Russia and France, 1885–98

Salisbury expected the settlement with Russia in September 1885 to provide no more than a breathing space. Russia would continue to improve its railway communications with Central Asia. In the Near East Britain's position was weaker than in 1878 as long as the Straits were closed to the Royal Navy. Russia's potential in Central Asia led Lord Roberts (the commander-in-chief in India) to argue in 1888 that if the British army failed to take the offensive against a Russian threat, this 'would destroy the confidence of the native army and civil population, and undermine our prestige and supremacy in the East'. His aim in 1891 was to establish a defensive line from Kabul to Kandahar in the event of a Russian advance. But this was no more than a theoretical solution. The logistics alone would have posed formidable problems. Pleas for reinforcements from Britain in the event of a crisis brought far from encouraging replies from London between 1888 and 1893. British officials in India also decided that they could not afford to enlarge their own army. Fortunately, for the time being the Russians seemed content to consolidate their position in Central Asia. They were becoming more interested in China and the Far East. A start was made to the building of the Trans-Siberian Railway in 1891.[10]

Meanwhile, defence issues in general had been exciting more interest in Britain from the 1880s. Some action was taken to implement the recommendations of the three reports of the Carnarvon Royal Commission on Imperial Defence (1881 and 1882). The aim was the creation of an imperial network of fortified ports and coaling stations. But the intensified colonial activities of other powers, the building of fast cruisers by France and Russia, and decreasing British naval confidence in the prevention of their escape by close blockade, suggested that the improvements were not keeping pace with the potential threat. The enhancement of national and imperial security was in any case hampered by the usual financial constraints, by inter-service jealousies and lack of co-operation, and by the virtual absence of the institutions and personnel needed to plan and attempt an overview. But at least a start was made during the decade to exchanges between the emerging army and navy intelligence departments.

In the early 1880s the navy, according to A. J. Marder,[11] was at its lowest level in terms of *matériel* since the mid eighteenth century. The Board of Admiralty was burdened by much routine business. There was no naval war staff or war college. A war would have found the service singularly ill prepared qualitatively as well as in numbers of ships. As early as September 1884 articles in the *Pall Mall Gazette* began to sound the alarm concerning the navy's decline in relation to its rivals. Some increase in naval spending followed.

The army, meanwhile, despite Cardwell's reforms in the early 1870s, had achieved no more than modest advances in its capabilities. The newly-created reserve of 80,000 soldiers at first merely filled the gaps in existing units in an emergency. The search for more and better recruits coincided with a shortage of volunteers. Nevertheless, a start was made in 1886 to the formation of an expeditionary force of two army corps on recognisably modern lines. Although problems persisted in administration and planning, some attention was at last being paid to the changing character of European armies as these tried to emulate the efficiency demonstrated by the Prussian army in 1870–1. In 1886, for instance, the director of military intelligence claimed, as French capabilities increased, that he might have only a week's warning of an invasion attempt against Britain.

In the Stanhope Memorandum of 1 June 1891, the assumption was made that 'the employment of an Army Corps in the field of any European war [was] sufficiently improbable' for this to be given a high priority. It was therefore 'the primary duty of the military authorities to organise our forces efficiently for the defence of this country'. The other tasks of the army were described as giving aid to the civil power at home and the defence of the empire. It reaffirmed that two corps were to be held in reserve in Britain to provide speedy relief in a crisis. But no government was willing to contemplate either controversial or expensive improvements.

Changes on the international stage also briefly diminished the sense of alarm, and suggested that there might still be scope for statecraft. This was important, given that Salisbury was in power for much of the period between 1885 and the end of the century. He took only a limited interest in defence questions, whereas he revelled in the mysteries of diplomacy. Above all, he could take advantage of the Austro-Russian Balkan differences which led to the break-up of the *Dreikaiserbund* from the summer of 1886. France's differences with Italy and Germany similarly supplied him with room for manoeuvre. Although an Italian proposal for an alliance against France was regarded as too binding, in 1887 Salisbury negotiated agreements for selective and limited co-operation with Rome (and later Vienna) to uphold the status quo in the Mediterranean. He saw that it made sense to try to offer reassurance of a kind to Austria-Hungary, lest that empire should feel driven to conclude some new deal with Russia.

Salisbury's primary concern, however, was that 'as little should happen as possible in that region'. The agreements pulled together vague promises of co-operation against either French or Russian aggressive moves in the Mediterranean, North Africa, Bulgaria, the Straits and Asia Minor. Salisbury also attempted something more positive, given his desire to defuse rivalries and tensions wherever possible. He made a final – though vain – attempt to negotiate a British withdrawal from Egypt.

These improvements to Britain's international position, however, were not sufficient in themselves. The Admiralty at this time could not reinforce the Mediterranean fleet to the level which would have made British policy in a crisis fully credible. Indeed, from 1888, with more and more talk of possible France-Russian naval cooperation, fears grew that the Royal Navy might find itself outnumbered in a war with those two powers. The Admiralty in consequence took as its first priority the protection of British interests from French attacks *outside* the Mediterranean, a sea it was prepared to abandon temporarily – if necessary – at the start of a war. The army joined in the demand for more men and weapons and put renewed emphasis on the danger of invasion.

Salisbury himself admitted that British naval policy in the Mediterranean was out of step with the diplomatic strategy he had adopted in conjuction with Italy and Austria. If the status quo in the region covered by the Mediterranean Agreements were seriously challenged, some time must elapse before Britain could intervene effectively with warships – let alone with troops. But suggestions for an alliance with Germany did not appeal to him. A reduction in Britain's future freedom of action seemed too high a price to pay. Salisbury was, in any case, reluctant to make any choice which finally closed the door to possible improvements in relations with France. Although he classified France (like Russia) as a 'hungry' power, this was offset by the interest of Germany as well as Austria-Hungary in the status quo.

He also claimed that the current state of home politics prevented the adoption of a bold foreign policy. Every British government – or so he said – had been reduced to 'absolute dependence on the *aura popularis*'. Nevertheless he cast around for some step that would enhance British credibility as a great power. The answer – naval expansion at a cost of £21.5 million – was not cheap, but it was the least controversial way forward. It was also a popular measure in some quarters, and it simultaneously promised more security and influence for Britain in the wider world as well as in European waters.[12]

The Naval Defence Act of March 1889 was the most ambitious effort since the early 1860s to strengthen the navy and the security of Britain and the empire. Warships, it was now argued, would be a better defence against invasion than more fortifications. Advances in technology and design meant that money could be spent with confidence on a new class of capital ship. The Treasury was even relatively flush with funds.[13] Parliament was told on 7 March 1889 that 'our establishment should be on such a scale that it should at least be equal to the naval strength of any two other countries'. The formulation of the two-power standard (the most specific aim was a force at least equal to any Franco-Russian combination in the Mediterranean) was a landmark in the history of the late-Victorian navy. Once articulated, it became a measure from which any government found it difficult to depart without giving an impression of weakness both at home and abroad. The principle of the two-power standard was confirmed in 1894 when Gladstone's cabinet colleagues stood out against his pleas to limit naval expenditure. His resignation effectively marked the end of the search for a distinctive Liberal foreign policy.

Paul Kennedy suggests that in many ways the race with Russia and France from 1889 was 'a more serious matter' for British naval mastery than that with Germany before 1914. There was a real danger that these two rivals might take the lead, especially in waters such as the Mediterranean or later in the Far East. In addition, the geographical spread of France and Russia made it impossible for the British to contain their battlefleets as easily as that of Germany in the North Sea. Nor did Britain achieve the 60 per cent lead over France and Russia which she later sustained against Tirpitz's 'risk-fleet'.[14]

If neither the French nor the Russian government from 1889 was in so dangerous a frame of mind as that of Germany before August 1914, a repeat of the kind of sequence of decisions and incidents which had led to the Crimean War could not be discounted. The British were also being confronted by the very challenge which their diplomats had striven so assiduously to avoid since 1815. The Mediterranean in particular, as A. J. Marder notes, remained 'England's Achilles' heel'. Yet it was here that the British believed that they had a crucial part to play in the maintenance of the peace of Europe. Only with a strong fleet could they demonstrate their support for Italy, Austria-Hungary and the status quo in the Mediterranean. Without naval supremacy, London would have little say in the future of the Ottoman Empire.[15] In addition, some 10 per cent of Britain's trade was with the countries of southern Europe. A further 16 per cent of Britain's exports and over 20 per cent of her imports used the Mediterranean–Suez Canal route. Suez was highly prized for the quickest movement of British forces to or from India and the Far East.

The Admiralty, however, was still not satisfied. It continued to

argue that strong squadrons were needed to protect British shipping along all the main routes. It particularly objected to naval
operations against Russia even if the Dardanelles were open to
allow British forces to take action in the Black Sea. The navy could
operate in the Near East only 'across the ruins of the French fleet'.
Indeed, given the danger that the Toulon fleet might escape into the
Atlantic and threaten various areas including the British Isles,
Gibraltar seemed the obvious point of naval concentration at the
start of any crisis.[16]

But where the admirals based their reasoning on how they would
fight a war, Salisbury was thinking in terms of a political struggle
for advantage in which war was an unlikely outcome. He believed
that as long as Britain was loosely aligned with the Central Powers
by way of Italy, they would not seek to return to the *Dreikaiserbund*.
Only through a revival of that three-power combination would
Russia have real power at the Straits. Others were less confident.
They included Salisbury's own nephew, Arthur Balfour, who was
beginning to make a mark as a student of grand strategy. He took
the possibility of war very seriously. In March 1892 he also insisted
that British use of the Straits was dependent upon the most comprehensive advance preparations, including 'transports etc. [i.e.
soldiers] being kept in constant readiness at Malta'.[17] Russia, he
believed, could easily win a race to control Constantinople.

Salisbury was not easily dissuaded. While he professed himself
no 'bigot' on the subject of Russia and Constantinople, he feared a
massive blow to Britain's honour and influence abroad if she failed
to support Turkey in a crisis. Her standing among the peoples of
India would be harmed. The Suez route might become unusable in
time of war.[18] But in 1895 another crisis in the Ottoman Empire
found the cabinet on the whole more responsive to the fears of the
Admiralty than to the views of the Prime Minister. The directors of
military and naval intelligence (DMI and DNI) expressed themselves forcefully on the question (see Document 15). Late in 1896
both argued strongly for a formidable British presence in Egypt.
This, they believed, should neutralise any threat from Russia
through the Straits, or from France via the Sudan.[19]

Turkish massacres of Armenians further weakened Salisbury's
position. The British public would no longer stomach a pro-Turkish
policy. Thus, in exchanges with Vienna in 1896–7, Salisbury found
himself unable to give a specific promise to defend Constantinople

against Russia. He could talk only of identity of interest. The Austrians, as it happened, were discovering that the Russians had become interested in the the status quo in the Near East (given their desire to pursue their ambitions in the Far East). Therefore, as Vienna and St Petersburg mended broken fences, Salisbury at last agreed that Britain should 'gradually' (and reluctantly) disengage from Constantinople. Egypt (with control of the Nile to its source) would have to become the new key to British strategy in the eastern Mediterranean.[20]

Good fortune and some astute diplomacy had already enabled Salisbury (in March 1896) to begin the conquest of the Sudan – something he had been contemplating since 1890. Once the old policy with respect to Turkey was no longer sustainable, Egypt had to be secured, even at the expense of conflict with France. In 1898, when the struggle for control of the Upper Nile reached its climax at Fashoda, it was the French who found themselves isolated (the Russians being preoccupied in Manchuria). France was compelled to accept all Britain's chief demands relating to the region. The Admiralty even had enough warships to concentrate the Mediterranean fleet at Malta to cover Egypt against any Russian threat. So confident were the admirals in this particular crisis that they feared their main problem might be the reluctance of the enemy battlefleets to give the British the opportunity to win a new Trafalgar. They had, however, yet to convince the politicians that the navy's hold on the Mediterranean required the creation of a third base at Alexandria.[21]

Defence and diplomacy at the turn of the century

Britain did not totally disinterest herself from the fate of the Ottoman Empire and the Straits, but the objective now was to minimise the benefits that Russia might derive from further advances and to save British face. The continuing extension of the Russian rail network into Central Asia meant that, even if feasible, British attacks in the Black Sea region would no longer 'so occupy her [Russian] military forces as to prevent her from concentrating upon the Afghan border'. British pressure on Persia was also ruled out, given the strong Russian presence in the north and its wider financial influences. The Committee of Imperial Defence later (in February 1903) tried to console itself with the thought that while the Russians would draw some benefit from the possession of Constantinople and the sole right to naval use of the Straits, this would not fundamentally alter the strategic situation in the Mediterranean.[22]

Meanwhile, Salisbury characteristically continued to pay attention to the weaknesses and distractions of Britain's rivals as well as their apparent strengths. Russia's link with France was admittedly a major problem, but the latter, he believed, was still influenced by too many long-standing fears of and hostility towards Germany to run great risks in rivalry with Britain. He was by no means convinced that Russia was as formidable and aggressive as she was often portrayed. Even Russia's growing interest in Manchuria had its advantages, given that this region was far removed from Britain's own activities in China (which were concentrated further south), while resources expended in Manchuria could not be used to threaten the north-west frontier of India. The world, in his view, was still a big place, with plenty of room for all. Although he had leant towards the Triple Alliance upon occasions, he was happiest when free to negotiate constructively with all the European powers. This was the policy of 'the free hand' – not 'splendid isolation'. Salisbury believed that Britain's position in the world and the current state of international rivalries made this a sound policy (see Document 16).

In foreign affairs he sought a balance between resources and commitments. He was well aware that a narrow line ran between excessive ambition and undue conciliation. Nor could policy abroad be pursued without regard to domestic political needs – not least the avoidance as far as possible of costly defence programmes and high taxes. Even during the Boer War his reluctance to spend on the army was apparent. The Secretary of State for War recorded that Salisbury was out-voted over an increase in defence spending only 'after an appeal such as he never made to the Cabinet in his life, and we all thought he would go'.[23] The Prime Minister in any case never devoted so much attention to defence matters as he did to foreign affairs (the Navy Defence Act of 1889 being the one major exception).

Both Salisbury and Rosebery (for the Liberals) could lay claim to some successes through their quest for accommodations with imperial rivals. Salisbury, for instance, balanced absolute firmness over the control of the Nile with conciliation of France in West Africa. Rosebery between 1892 and 1895 had been able to work out a compromise with the Russians in the Pamirs Question (though the Russians might have thought their own position strong enough for them to appear generous).[24] The Tsar was also anxious not to drive the British closer to the Triple Alliance. Salisbury, for his part, was eager to negotiate with Russia to clarify and delimit spheres of influence and interest – notably in China. At the same time he thought that Britain was entitled to improve her communications with the south-eastern corner of Persia for commercial and strategic reasons.

Policy-makers, however, in Berlin and Vienna were inclined to take more note of his eagerness to conciliate. Britain's obvious readiness to compromise could raise doubts concerning her potential value as an ally.[25] Salisbury's policies also disturbed some of his own colleagues, notably Joseph Chamberlain. The latter believed that Britain's vulnerability needed to be offset by an alliance with Germany (or the United States). Salisbury, however, was more conscious of the costs than the advantages of a commitment to a continental power such as Germany.

But even Salisbury was prepared if necessary to take a tough line with the Boer Republics in South Africa. At the level of high politics the British feared for their influence at the Cape if the republics themselves became too rich, confident and assertive. They might establish ties with other imperial powers. The Cape route was still important in itself, and would be indispensable if Egypt and Suez were, for some reason, lost or isolated. But war, when it came, proved much more costly and difficult than the British had expected. The early defeats and the extent to which the conflict soaked up military and financial strength all gave rise to nervous questioning of past assumptions. Leo Amery bluntly said of the army of 1899 that as 'a fighting machine it was largely a sham'. It was too small, inadequately trained, and organised on no definitely thought out principle of imperial defence.

At least Salisbury's faith in the inability of the other powers to sink their differences and unite against Britain was vindicated during this war – although the Russians did float the idea of a continental coalition to put pressure on Britain. The French were certainly eager to help strengthen their ally in Central Asia. In contrast, the Germans feared that France and Russia would be the main beneficiaries from any such action to weaken the British Empire. Yet the British need to concentrate so many troops in South

Africa compounded the fears for the safety of India. British credibility as a power was damaged, while the Treasury fretted over the implications of the huge financial costs. Salisbury's colleagues concluded that tougher foreign, imperial and defence policies would be necessary for survival in a new century. To begin with there had to be a thorough review of the institutions responsible for defence and grand strategy.

As we have seen, unease over the adequacy of these institutions had arisen before. An invasion scare in 1888 led to the Hartington Commission. This reported in 1890 on the inadequacy of inter-service co-ordination. It called for a 'Naval and Military Council' to oversee imperial defence. It favoured the abolition of the commander-in-chief and the establishment of a War Office council and a modern general staff. Yet in practice successive ministries in the 1890s did no more than tinker with the problems. An advisory defence committee met occasionally under the chairmanship of the Lord President of the council (not the Prime Minister, who alone could have invested it with real influence). It included neither of the service chiefs, and kept no proper records. The War Office remained an 'augean stable'.[26] Balfour, alone among the leading politicians, attempted to think in broad terms concerning defence, but he could achieve little until he succeeded to the premiership in 1902. He was left to marvel at the readiness of the Victorians to trust the defence of Britain's vast economic interests in the world to such small forces.

Notes

1 R. Millman, *Britain and the Eastern Question, 1875–1878*, Oxford, 1979, pp. 107–8, 453, and see generally for the crisis of 1875–8.

2 *Ibid.*, p. 192.

3 R. Blake, *Disraeli*, London, 1966, pp. 577–87.

4 Millman, *Eastern Question*, pp. 307–11; W. F. Monypenny and G. E. Buckle, *The Life of Benjamin Disraeli*, London, 1910–20, vi, pp. 152, 155, 172.

5 Millman, *Eastern Question*, pp. 340–1, 389; Monypenny, *Disraeli*, vi. 246, 255–6.

6 Millman, *Eastern Question*, pp. 412–13, 416–17; B. H. Sumner, *Russia and the Balkans, 1870–80*, Oxford, 1937, pp. 420–4.

7 Southgate, *Palmerston*, pp. 539–40 and n.; Steele, *Palmerston*, pp. 287–8.

8   Ramm, *Correspondence*, i. 156.

9   Monypenny, *Disraeli*, vi. 434–5; Gillard, *Asia*, p. 136; M. T. Florinsky, *Russia: a history and interpretation*, New York, 1953, ii. 986.

10   A. L. Friedberg, *The Weary Titan: Britain and the experience of relative decline*, 1895–1905, Princeton, 1988, pp. 216–31.

11   A. J. Marder, *The Anatomy of British Sea Power, 1880–1905*, New York, 1940, p. 132, and see *passim* for naval issues.

12   See C. J. Lowe, *Salisbury and the Mediterranean, 1884–1896*, London, 1965, chapter 2.

13   See Sumida, *Naval Supremacy*, pp. 10–12 for the navy in the 1870s and 1880s.

14   P. Kennedy, *Strategy and Diplomacy, 1870–1914*, London, 1984, pp. 167–8.

15   Marder, *Anatomy*, pp. 145, 162.

16   *Ibid.*, pp. 144, 155; Lowe, *Salisbury*, p. 88; R. L. Greaves, *Persia and the Defence of India, 1884–1902*, London, 1959, pp. 215–16.

17   Lowe, *Salisbury*, p. 90; R. F. Mackay, *Balfour: intellectual statesman*, Oxford, 1985, pp. 64–5.

18   Greaves, *Persia*, pp. 217–18.

19   Marder, *Anatomy*, pp. 569–80.

20   Bourne, *Foreign Policy*, p. 452.

21   Marder, *Anatomy*, pp. 326–8.

22   Friedberg, *Weary Titan*, pp. 216–17; G. P. Gooch and H. W. V. Temperley, *British Documents on the Origins of the War, 1898–1914*, London, 1926–38, iv. 59–60.

23   E. M. Spiers, *Haldane: an army reformer*, Edinburgh, 1980, p. 50.

24   Gillard, *Asia*, pp. 155–6.

25   Lowe, *Salisbury*, pp. 93–8.

26   Mackay, *Balfour*, pp. 61–2; Friedberg, *Weary Titan*, pp. 209–12.

5

New threats, new policies
1901–14

The first reappraisals, 1901–4

The new century opened with the British government reflecting not
only on the painful lessons of the South African War, but also on
the influence of Russia in Persia and its continuing threat to the
north-west frontier of India (see Document 17). The Admiralty was
still troubled by the strength of the Russian and French navies (in
the Far East now, rather than the Mediterranean). The German fleet
was becoming strong enough to attract attention. Ministers were
soon convinced that radical changes were necessary both in foreign
and defence policies. The sense of urgency was intensified by the
continuing high level of spending on the armed forces even after
the defeat of the Boers. This could deprive the British of their 'great
reserve in time of war' – that is, the capacity to raise taxes and loans
more easily than their rivals.

Yet even the current expenditures did not provide sufficient
security. On 8 August 1902 Balfour, soon after he became Prime
Minister, bleakly told the Commons that India could no longer take
care of itself militarily, nor could Britain rely solely on the navy for
the defence of the trade routes or indeed the homeland. 'The problem of Imperial defence is one of the most difficult and one of the
most complicated problems that any Government or any body of
experts, can face . . .'. It presented immense 'intellectual and specu-
lative challenges'.[1]

In the *post mortems* which accompanied and followed the Boer
War, fault was found with the politicians as well as with the

generals. Both suffered from the shortage of information on which to base a war policy.[2] Planners were needed who would be kept fully supplied with assessments of the state of Britain's armed forces and of their ability to meet specific foreign threats. Overall there was an obvious need for a more coherent, integrated policy-making structure.

The Boer War had also provided a painful reminder of Britain's small numbers of trained reserves compared with those possessed by the European powers. The war had depleted garrisons in India as well as at home, despite volunteers from the British Isles and around the empire. The list of weaknesses could easily be extended. A leading British scholar has recently summed up the army's performance in one word – 'dismal'.[3] H. Arnold-Forster as Secretary of State for War in 1904 bluntly stated that the army 'in its present form' was not 'suited to the requirements of the country or adapted for war'. Yet efforts at reform in the early 1900s ran into intractable opposition from the Treasury, the War Office Council and some Unionist backbenchers.

Some progress was made elsewhere.[4] Of particular interest was the establishment of the Committee of Imperial Defence (CID), an inter-departmental body to advise on grand strategy and related matters. The hope was that, through a combination of permanent and flexible membership of ministers and professionals, defence policy would become better understood and better co-ordinated than in the past. The Admiralty and War Office should no longer be left to act as if they served different countries. In practice the new CID acquired no executive authority. Its role remained advisory. It did not become a centre for 'strategic planning' and failed to bridge fundamental inter-service differences and rivalries. Its views were not always acted upon. But at least it was a flexible and open body which could draw upon the advice of many experts.

The War Office was remodelled. It was now topped by a strong Army Council somewhat akin to the Board of Admiralty. This was presided over by the Secretary of State for War. A start was made to the creation of a General Staff. The position of commander-in-chief was at last abolished, and by end of 1905 the Army Council was beginning to develop into an institution which could supply 'specialist military advice on all the various aspects of organising a modern army'. Richard Haldane, the new Liberal Secretary of State for War from the end of 1905, was greatly assisted by these reforms.

He was also in the happy position of being able to learn from the mistakes and frustrations of his predecessors.

The first practical steps to ease the burdens on Britain's defence forces began as early as 1901–2. Despite the existence of the two-power standard, the Admiralty was still short of the strength it deemed appropriate. Selborne, the First Lord of the Admiralty, argued in December 1900 that while the 'aggregate of the French and Russian Navies governs the number of our ships', he was 'inclined to think that we shall be liable to be blackmailed by our "friends" if we give ourselves no margin'. But in 1901 the cabinet decided that Britain could afford to build against only two enemies, and that naval policy should be based on the assumption of friendship with, or the neutrality of, Germany, Italy, Japan and the United States. Selborne himself admitted that the two-power standard could no longer be automatically determined by the size of the next two largest fleets. The United States could, if it wished, easily build the world's largest navy.[5] Fortunately, progress was being made in talks to improve relations with that country. The British had reason to hope that they would be spared significant defence commitments in the New World.

Success here, however, would still leave the navy overstretched. The Admiralty feared in particular that it would be unable to match a Franco-Russian naval combination in the Far East. An alliance with Japan, another rising naval power, began to have its attractions. The Foreign Office reached the same conclusion in 1901, but only after its efforts to negotiate with other powers had come to nothing. Neither Germany nor the United States would support Britain in the Far East. Under the terms of the alliance of 30 January 1902, Britain still promised if possible to deploy a naval force superior to any third party in the Far East, while the alliance did nothing directly to improve Britain's position on the north-west frontier of India. Japan, however, could be expected to try to turn any Russo-British collision to its advantage in Korea and South Manchuria, as well as to exert influence with its navy.

Balfour continued to reflect on the interconnectedness of British strategy. Asia and Europe interacted. In December 1901 he insisted that any conflict in the East was likely to spread to the English Channel and the Mediterranean. Britain's interests were consequently bound up with the survival of the Triple Alliance led by Germany. It should not be crushed between 'the hammer of Russia and the anvil of France'.[6] Moreover, since Fashoda the Franco-Russian alliance had taken on a markedly anti-British tendency, with French capital, for instance, helping to fund Russian railway building in Central Asia.

India, however, remained the chief preoccupation of the CID in its first years, interrupted by occasional reference to the old subject of invasion threats to Britain. There was renewed talk of India's need for a 'continental' army to meet a continental threat. The War Office commented in 1901: 'Speaking broadly, so long as the Navy fulfils its mission, the British Empire is impervious to the great land forces except in one point – India. . . . The loss of India . . . would be a death-blow to our prosperity, prestige and power.' At least, as Selborne noted, better relations with the United States and the defeat of the Boers had disposed of Britain's other 'military frontiers' with land powers.[7]

India's strategic, political and economic importance made its loss unthinkable to most people. Although a modern scholar has suggested that it 'was less the jewel in the imperial crown than a crown of thorns', it might more appropriately be described as both.[8] Lord Curzon, the Viceroy of India, believed that Britain had to demonstrate unequivocally that it was not Russia's 'irresistible destiny' to secure the Persian Gulf and Kabul (see also Document 17). But his proposed counter-strokes had already caused Lord Salisbury to protest that the Viceroy wanted him to talk to Russia 'as if I had five hundred thousand men at my back, and I do not'. Balfour's cabinet was equally constrained.[9] Nevertheless the British could hardly feel comfortable as long as they were vulnerable and the Russians were not. Even Salisbury had calculated in 1900 that without a railway to Seistan the British might be unable to find a tenable defensive line other than on the frontier of India itself. More particularly he feared that St Petersburg at some time would use the threat to India to force the British to acknowledge that Russia was 'mistress of the greater part of China'.

But the circulation of paper after paper merely appeared to prove that a solution to the defence of India might be impossible with the forces that Britain could realistically hope to muster. The Secretary to the CID in 1904 finally rebelled against the 'academic' prophets of doom. One had to plan on the the basis of what Britain could afford – not pursue idle dreams. The Russians, too, would experience enormous problems if they tried to advance. Others agreed that British spies in Central Asia should provide ample warning, given the scale of the preparations which would precede a drive deep into Afghanistan. This did not silence General Kitchener (now commanding in India), who continued to call for at least 100,000 reinforcements in the first six months of an emergency on the northwest frontier (a figure he later raised by another 50,000).

Balfour finally closed the matter by swinging behind the pragmatists. Britain could not meet every threat. Priorities had to be established on the basis of actual – not ideal – numbers of soldiers. In the first place he instructed the CID to try to clarify the seriousness of the invasion threat to Britain once and for all. It concluded that the navy should have sufficient warning to counter an invasion attempt, provided an enemy were compelled (by the strength of the land forces in Britain) to send at least 70,000 troops. With one 'great' regular division, the auxiliary forces, and a navy built to the two-power standard plus a 10 per cent margin in battleships, the British homeland should be safe.

Even this verdict failed to produce more than 100,000 troops which could be sent to India in the first year of a war. It was hoped, however, that reinforcements on this scale would enable the army of India to hold a line from Kabul to Kandahar as proposed earlier by Roberts. But if this was progress, it was balanced by the growing claims of a third critical area: Egypt.

The cabinet was not tempted by suggestions from the Army Council that the outbreak of the Russo-Japanese War in February 1904 might be the time to challenge Russia in Central Asia. The Treasury had recently warned that in the present state of Britain's finances a great war could be fought only at 'an absolutely ruinous cost'. Balfour in any case believed that Britain could not raise the troops required to fight a major war. The Russo-Japanese War, however, provided unexpected relief. Contrary to most expectations, the Japanese not only won the war, but did so by a wide margin. Revolution also broke out in Russia. Nevertheless, the British government was still sufficiently pessimistic to negotiate an extension to the Anglo-Japanese alliance in 1905. In future, not only would this operate against a single belligerent, but it would extend to the defence of India (see Document 18).

Enter Germany

Germany had often been a subject of British complaint since 1871, but it was not until the early 1900s that persistent and serious differences developed between the two powers. Balfour commented in April 1902 that Anglo-German interests – 'broadly speaking' – were 'identical'. He did, however, concede even then that, while he doubted the existence of a threat, logic might not prevail. The Admiralty had begun to pay some attention to the rise of Germany as a naval power from the late 1890s.[10] Admiral Tirpitz's basic aim was to create a fleet strong enough to give Germany bargaining power over Britain after the latter's navy had been weakened in what was assumed to be an inevitable (though victorious) war with France and Russia. As a counter to this, the Admiralty from 1902 pressed for the two-power standard plus an extra six battleships over and above straight parity with France and Russia. In a cabinet memorandum of 26 February 1904, the First Lord claimed that the German navy was being 'carefully built up from the point of view of a war with us'.

There were other signs of fear of or hostility towards Germany. Joseph Chamberlain, for instance, successfully mobilised opinion against his cabinet colleagues and the War Office when they were tempted to welcome the the German-inspired Berlin to Baghdad Railway as a potential obstacle to Russian penetration of the Middle East. But even in 1903–4, when the British were negotiating the *entente* with France, most of the leading figures were still not (or were only partially) influenced by fear of Germany. Their main concern was to free themselves as far as possible from various colonial and imperial difficulties with France. In particular, the British were now willing to grant the French a free hand in Morocco in return for similar freedom for themselves in Egypt. Their fears over a military threat to the eight-mile-wide entrance to the Mediterranean were allayed by the French agreement that if Morocco were occupied, the coastline in question would pass to Spain and would be left unfortified. The approach and onset of the Russo-Japanese War gave both powers an incentive to accelerate the talks in order to lessen the danger of being drawn into the conflict by their respective allies.

The conclusion of the *entente* in April 1904, however, did not immediately put an end to the Admiralty's inclusion of France in the plans for 'every possible naval war'. The famous fleet redistribution scheme at the end of the year was not simply prompted by fear of Germany. Ruddock Mackay shows that it was designed to safeguard British interests in the Mediterranean as well as in the North Sea. As Admiral Sir John Fisher later declared, the fleet positioned at Gibraltar would be able to 'turn the scale' in support of ships based at Dover or Malta. A start was finally made in 1905 to the long-sought-after base at Alexandria.

The successive blows to the Russian fleet at the hands of the Japanese in 1904–5 meant that the German navy moved up to partner France in setting the two-power standard. It was in 1905 that Germany came incontrovertibly to the forefront when it not only tried to assert itself in Morocco, but was seemingly intent on humiliating France and breaking the new *entente*. Even then the Admiralty continued to stress the 'kaleidoscopic nature' of international relations, insisting in February 1906 that battleships were surer 'pledges' of future security than *ententes*. By this time the drastic naval reform programmes directed by Fisher as First Sea Lord were in full swing, while the concentration of most of the fleet in European (soon to become northern European) waters was accelerating.

The decimation of the distant squadrons, and the scrapping of obsolescent vessels did not pass unchallenged. Sir John Colomb, for instance, asked Parliament in March 1905 whether Britain would always be able to rely on the friendship of the United States and Japan. He noted that Britain's Far Eastern interests were as yet unsupported by a major naval base. But Colomb was asking for too much at that time. Even the building of the new North Sea base at Rosyth proceeded slowly. It was far from complete in August 1914. Britain could no longer aspire to relative safety in almost every region of the world.

It is true that, briefly, with the destruction of two out of three of Russia's fleets, Britain's position at sea was stronger than it had been for a generation. But it would not be long before great efforts would be needed to keep a healthy lead over Germany. Furthermore, this temporary relief in naval competition was offset by the major change in the balance in Europe as a result of Russia's defeat and the revolution of 1905. The German leadership, confident of a clear military advantage over France, tried to exploit the situation, not only to enhance their interests in Morocco, but also to underline French vulnerability and relative isolation in Europe.

The suspicions of the British government were soon aroused. A sub-committee of strategic experts advised – as tension mounted between Berlin and Paris – that if Germany were to overthrow France, this would upset the European balance of power to such an extent that it might 'be necessary for Great Britain in her own interest to lend France her active support' from the start of any war.[11] Lansdowne, while he hoped in his remaining months as Foreign Secretary to avoid a permanent rift with Germany, agreed that France had to be strongly supported in the present crisis. The right signals had to be sent to both Paris and Berlin, though in the case of France this meant support which fell short of a precise commitment. Britain, he warned Paris, would fight only in 'certain eventualities' when British interests were under direct threat.

Both services were now thinking seriously of just such an eventuality. Indeed the army, despite Salisbury's verdict in 1902 that intervention to defend Belgian neutrality was too hypothetical a question to deserve consideration, had already given some thought to action on the Continent. From August 1905 it proceeded to examine in more detail how 70,000 troops might be sent to Belgium at short notice. The Admiralty, too, was active. Naturally it believed that the navy should have the primary role. Germany's north-west coast was designated the appropriate theatre for offensive operations on land. Not surprisingly, attempts to co-ordinate the two services merely highlighted their differences and discouraged co-operation. The CID could neither give orders nor arbitrate.[12]

Balfour's cabinet, meanwhile, was distracted by domestic problems. Abroad it was devoting much time to the renewal and extension of the Anglo-Japanese alliance. It was not entirely sure of France's capacity or will to resist German pressure, especially given the plight of its Russian ally. Indeed, a Russo-German alignment was considered possible in the summer of 1905. Lansdowne wished to do no more than was strictly necessary to protect British interests and standing. The new Liberal cabinet which took office in December might have been expected to be equally or more cautious.

As it happened Sir Edward Grey, the new Foreign Secretary, had definite views of his own. He had strong supporters in key places – including the Foreign and War Offices. With the assent of the Prime Minister, he was able to implement a more consistently anti-German line. Grey believed that the balance of power in Europe was in jeopardy due to Russia's revolution and setbacks in the Far

East. Any sign of weakness by Britain at this juncture would damage her credibility in the eyes of *all* the powers. On the other hand, a strong British stand might restrain the Germans and even help to persuade the Russians to come to a 'friendly agreement' over Persia and Afghanistan. British imperial interests and concern for the balance in Europe were thus intertwined. This thinking was strongly supported by a new generation of officials in the Foreign Office: men who believed that the methods and thinking of Salisbury were out of date. Britain could no longer be so confident that the other powers would tend to cancel each other out.

Highly secret staff talks were conducted with the French in the middle of December 1905. Some diplomats and naval officers were also involved, but most members of the Liberal cabinet were unaware of what was happening. Grey himself claimed that the talks did not commit Britain in any way. At the same time he thought it vital to stiffen French resolve and preserve the *entente*. If Britain were involved in a land war in Europe, he expected her role to be very small.[13] He was well aware that his own party was vehemently opposed to any form of compulsory service.

The General Staff, meanwhile, was persuading itself that an 'efficient army' of 120,000 might just tip the balance in favour of French survival in a war with Germany. It was calculated that Germany, once it had been defeated at sea, might soon come to feel itself 'impotent on land'.[14] In fact, the Germans in 1906 were supremely confident of victory against France in the event of war. Their diplomatic defeats at the Algeciras Conference over the future of Morocco came as an unpleasant shock. Meanwhile, British planners continued to be excited by the new challenge, and perhaps found it a more satisfying experience that the long and seemingly fruitless quest for an answer to the Russian threat from Central Asia.

Military reform and war in Europe

It was a Liberal government, many of whose members were strongly opposed to huge armaments, which – ironically – did much to improve the effectiveness of the army. With respect to the policy of the previous government, Edward Spiers has remarked. 'Not only had it failed to marry the objectives of army reform and a reduction in military spending, but it had failed, above all, to produce a composite reform of the regular and auxiliary forces.'[15] Richard Haldane, the Liberal Secretary of State for War, also faced major problems with ministerial colleagues, his own party, and a somewhat confused and demoralised War Office. He could, however, impress the generals with the argument that life for them would be even more difficult under any other Liberal Secretary of State.

Haldane recognised the need for economy as well as efficiency. As Spiers notes, a minister 'could not reform the army for war *per se*, he could only reform the army within the limits imposed . . . by a peacetime government.' He had to reconcile short- and long-term needs, and do so within the constraints imposed by national preferences and prejudices. 'Economy and not Europe . . . [was] the *sine qua non* of Haldane's army reform.'[16] The army was exposed to a Fisher-like search for dead-wood, and to close questioning as to its purpose. Haldane's prime object was the creation of a substantial home-based striking force to meet foreign emergencies, the want of which had been so evident in various crises from the Crimean War.

The need for this was highlighted within days of his taking office. He was warned by Grey on 8 January 1906 that Germany might attack France inside a matter of months. Haldane discovered that it would take at least eight weeks to muster an expeditionary force of no more than 80,000 troops. Britain needed a force which could be sent, 'with the least possible delay, to any part of the world'. Vital as was the stimulus provided by possible military involvement in Europe in 1906, some thought continued to be given to the defence of India. But this became increasingly difficult to sustain as Germany attracted more and more attention. Russia's weakness and its *entente* with Britain in 1907 also reduced the sense of urgency on the north-west frontier.

In practice it was found that, with the most skilful shuffling of the potential manpower (a quarter of a million regulars, plus reserves and auxiliaries), a force of some 150,000 men was the largest which could be organised after all the other inescapable commitments of the army had been met. Haldane could only hope that this would prove equal to whatever task it was called upon to perform. At the same time the planners had to accept that such an expeditionary force, once put in the field, would require speedy and regular reinforcements. Only some form of compulsory service would have made this possible. But the Liberals, fearful of a party split, torpedoed even tentative talks with the Unionists on this subject.[17]

The 'brains' of the army were also being developed. The Unionists had made a start to the creation of a General Staff. As one expert commented, 'Pieces of the framework of a General Staff had been juxtaposed awaiting the arrival of someone to fit them together.' This was done early in the Haldane era. The completion of the expeditionary force took much longer. It was not until May 1914 that General Sir Henry Wilson (Director of Military Operations from 1910) seemed reasonably satisfied with the plans and preparations to mobilise the army for war. A perfectionist, he privately recorded his real feelings early in 1913, which were that the 'best guarantee for the preservation of the peace of Europe would be a British army proportionate to our population, our pretensions and our wealth'.

The Anglo-French staff talks proceeded on an infrequent basis until 1910, so that the government in Paris remained far from confident that British backing would be forthcoming in a crisis. Its worries increased in the spring of 1909 when the Bosnian affair caused a brief crisis between the eastern powers. Germany and Austria were able to humiliate Russia and Serbia. Grey, conscious of the limitations of the *ententes* and how little he had to offer in the power game, tried to impress the Russians with a flurry of diplomatic activity in Vienna. But he was unable to persuade the Austrians to lessen their pressure on Belgrade. Nor did he find it easy to persuade advocates of full-scale alliances with France and Russia that they were asking for the moon.

Meanwhile, there had been only modest and ineffectual attempts to co-ordinate British naval and military planning.[18] Not even the CID could overcome the lack of inter-service co-operation, or – in the view of some critics – instil the necessary urgency into British thinking at the highest level. Military talks with the French made progress on questions of logistics, but not on the objectives of the expeditionary force itself. Grey continued to profess his ignorance of what was being discussed by the military. It has been argued that this 'negated much of his prudent approach to Anglo-French relations' – he was failing to supervise the military talks. These talks – with Henry Wilson in the lead – were becoming increasingly detailed and far-reaching.[19] Asquith as Prime Minister remained in the background. Yet one might reasonably ask whether British interests were sufficiently under threat to require new political action, until Franco-German rivalry in Morocco led to a new crisis with the arrival of a German gunboat at Agadir on 1 July 1911.

In response to this crisis, even the radicals agreed that some diplomatic support should be given to France. At the same time they required reassurance with a show of even-handedness towards Germany. Thus the cabinet, to the disgust of Paris and Grey's professional advisers, talked of offering Germany an unfortified port in Morocco. The Foreign Office warned that such a gesture might cause France to lose confidence in Britain. But ministers had to consider the unity of their party. Grey did his best to square the circle. On the one hand he was advising ministerial colleagues that France must not be allowed to feel let down by Britain (her own Mediterranean interests might suffer in consequence); on the other, he was instructing his ambassador in Paris that Britain could not go to war to give France possession of Morocco. He wrote: 'if we go to war it must be in defence of British interests'.[20] Grey could feel that his ambiguity was justified when German policy began to moderate not long afterwards.

Although the Agadir crisis (as will be explained later) had some effect on British defence thinking, it still failed to clarify the political position of Britain towards France. For all Grey's efforts, the unity of the cabinet remained precarious. At a discussion of the Anglo-French staff talks in November 1911, Grey, supported by Asquith, did his best to argue that Britain was not politically committed. Indeed, he tried to claim that the talks actually increased her freedom of action. They ensured that Britain could intervene more effectively and quickly – but only if and when she chose to do so. The fact remained, however, that Grey could not fully satisfy either the radicals or the French. The latter were unsure whether the British would act in an emergency, and they continued to be unimpressed by the size of the expeditionary force.

But if key ministers understandably recoiled at this stage from risking the unity of the Liberal Party, they had the authority (and it was their duty) to end the damaging army–navy split over strategy. Hitherto the navy had stubbornly ignored the soldiers' demands for assistance and protection as they prepared for their hypothetical dash across the Channel. But at a meeting of the CID on 23 August 1911 (prompted by the Agadir crisis) ministers at last realised that the two services could not be left to plan for two separate wars.

S. R. Williamson scathingly and rightly comments, 'The politics of grand strategy were often the politics of personal and service ambition, slightly tempered by concern for national interests.'[21]

The navy, in putting its case to the CID in August, simplistically stated that the first objective in a war must be the destruction of the enemy fleet. It clung tenaciously to its argument that the army should be deployed at home or used to threaten the coast of northern Germany. The Admiralty, it seemed, was unable to come to terms with the implications if Britain decided to support France in a war against Germany. In contrast, the army's case was argued with great fluency by Henry Wilson.

Ten days earlier the General Staff had elaborated in one interesting memorandum arguments which they had been developing since at least 1905 (see Document 23). Germany, it was said, might be making a bid for hegemony on lines last attempted by Napoleon. Britain's choices in the event of war were to back France or remain neutral. If she held aloof she had to face the probability of France's defeat – even if Russia was at war with Germany in the east. Such an outcome would be highly damaging to Britain. The British expeditionary force, small as it was, would have a moral as well as a material effect on the Continent.

The memorandum honestly conceded that 'the result in the opening moves [of a campaign] might be doubtful', but hopes were pinned on the prevention of a quick German victory. The longer the war went on, the greater the strain that would be imposed on Germany – especially once the naval blockade began to bite. The same paper also correctly anticipated that the weaker German fleet would stand on the defensive, and make use of mines and submarines rather than risk battle in the North Sea as the Admiralty expected and hoped. This document (irrespective of defects in specific details, or the fear of some leading generals that the expeditionary force was too weak to influence the outcome in France) was based on sensible assumptions, and these were backed up with a clear statement of the relationships between the land and sea campaigns.[22]

It was on these lines that Wilson argued to such effect at the CID meeting of 23 August 1911. Williamson describes this as the committee's 'only excursion before 1914 into the realm of grand strategy and overall strategic coordination'. The earlier failure of the Prime Minister – for whatever reasons – to intervene had left the Admiralty free to go its own way. Asquith now accepted the General Staff's proposals, although only 'in principle' and on the rather unenthusiastic ground that they were the only possible alternative to the 'puerile' ideas of the sailors. He was still reluctant to countenance the speedy dispatch of the expeditionary force to take part in a continental war. Yet if Wilson had not won outright, the Admiralty had clearly lost. Ministers were so unimpressed and even dismayed by the Admiralty's arguments that they decided to create a naval war staff to put some substance into its planning. Under Churchill as the new First Lord, an inter-service dialogue of sorts at last began to develop on the implications of intervention on the side of France.[23]

Historians have not found it difficult to criticise the Liberal government as it tried nervously to hedge its bets at home and abroad. Williamson argues that Asquith himself probably failed to realise that the military talks committed Britain to 'a particular strategy of such magnitude as to constitute a political decision'. While he was able to hold his cabinet together with assurances that the nation's treaty obligations contained no secret arrangements, the government became increasingly – and 'perhaps unwittingly' – committed to a continental strategy.[24] This turned out to be the case, but to such charges Asquith might have replied that until August 1914 (when war in Europe became a fact as opposed to a possibility), the unity of his cabinet and party, and various issues affecting the future of the British Isles, had to be given a higher priority. As a golfer, he was content to play one hole at a time.

The naval race and Anglo-German relations, 1908–14

The naval race was the most persistent and the most publicised issue in Anglo-German relations in the years before the outbreak of the First World War. But it must also be seen in the context of government fears of German hegemony in Europe. It was by that road, rather than in direct collision with the British navy, that Germany was expected by the best-informed to pose the main threat to national security. Thus, the first Anglo-French staff talks antedated the start of the truly acute period of Anglo-German naval antagonism. Furthermore, in the matter of the naval race the British were in familiar and seemingly predictable waters. Though costly and not without its periods of tension, it was a race which the

British were broadly confident of winning – so long as Germany was the only real challenger. Tirpitz himself repeatedly conceded the strength of the British position. In contrast, the British were ill equipped to participate in a continental war. At best they could hope that, if at the start the outcome was finely balanced in France and Belgium, their expeditionary force might tip the scales against Germany.

Britain's naval advantages in 1906–7 were such that the Liberals were temporarily able to slow capital ship construction. This feeling of security permitted Grey to examine the possibility of naval limitation agreements. As in the past, it was in Britain's self interest to attempt to reduce international tension and competition. Grey could also use the talks to try to placate the radicals (given their hostility to huge armaments). In practice these and later conversations with Germany demonstrated that progress was either impossible, or could only be achieved if Britain promised to remain neutral in a European war. For Grey and the Foreign Office this was unthinkable. To make such a concession would increase Germany's bargaining power in peace, as well as improve the chances of its victory in a continental war. Nor did they wish to forfeit French and Russian respect and risk a return to the problems of the era before the *ententes*. Britain's overall position in the world had become too exposed to risk 'isolation'.

Good relations with the United States and Japan, plus naval supremacy in northern European waters as well as the *ententes* thus formed the heart of British strategy before 1914. But to complete its credibility the British badly needed a revival of Russian military power in Europe to create a stable balance. When completed, this might also compel the Germans to give a higher priority to their army and so restrict spending on their fleet. The flaw in this strategy was that Berlin might resort to desperate measures before such a stalemate on land could be achieved. Shortly before the outbreak of war in 1914, one or two of the British leaders showed some awareness of this danger.

The most important of the domestic controversies over the navy occurred in 1909. This was an illuminating demonstration of the ease with which the admirals, the Unionists, and others who distrusted Liberal naval policy could mobilise popular support for an expanded capital ship programme. The crisis arose as a result of cabinet divisions over dreadnought building for that year. Such was the outcry that the ministerial debate was speedily resolved in favour of the expansionists. As Churchill put it, ministers who could not agree whether to authorise four or six new capital ships finally compromised by building eight.

Even so, the Admiralty from 1906–7 found it necessary to concentrate more and more of the fleet in home waters. But this further depletion of the foreign stations soon provoked strong protests from the Foreign Office. The latter asserted that, assuming the continuation of such a distribution, 'the only possible conclusion' must be that 'the exigencies of British world-wide policy and interests, in the present and immediate future' were being sacrificed to achieve a defensive concentration against an attack which was 'not likely to be made for some years to come'. The matter resurfaced more dramatically in 1912 over the future of British naval policy in the Mediterranean.[25]

The importance of the Mediterranean in British foreign and defence policy has demanded much attention in earlier sections of this study. As early as 1908, with the rise of the German menace in the North Sea, naval planners began to assume that the six remaining battleships in the Mediterranean would have to be recalled in the event of war. By 1912 it was also necessary to take account of the modernisation of the Austro-Hungarian fleet. There was uncertainty, too, as to how the Italians (normally assumed to be friendly or neutral) would behave in a crisis. The British had to ask themselves if they could afford to station enough ships to uphold their policy and pretensions in the Mediterranean.

Lord Esher, an influential but shadowy figure in British policy-making, thought that withdrawal would be interpreted as a signal of abdication as a world power. The Foreign Office argued that Italy, without the expectation of British naval assistance, might once again lean towards Germany and Austria-Hungary. They also feared a decline in British influence in Spain; Turkey might become a German client; even Britain's hold on Egypt might be weakened. Indeed, the ripples might spread as far afield as India. Churchill retorted on behalf of the Admiralty that provided Britain won 'the big battle in the decisive theatre' everything else could be put straight afterwards.[26]

The issue was not easily resolved. Suggestions for a deal whereby the French would concentrate their fleet in the Mediterranean were dismissed as demeaning, or as leading towards a formal alliance (or some other quid pro quo to satisfy the French). R. McKenna (a former Liberal First Lord) even preferred the expense of a larger fleet to dependence on a European ally. The radicals, who feared that Britain was already too committed to France, protested that any understanding would intensify the division of the European powers into two armed camps. Britain would be more likely to intervene on the side of France. On the other hand they were not willing to approve an increase in the naval estimates. In the end the decision that consultations with France provided the cheapest and quickest solution was qualified by an agreement to station a battle cruiser squadron at Malta – a force whose speed would enable it to refuse action if prudence dictated. But Grey, despite this new understanding and the continuing staff talks, felt obliged to warn the French ambassador on 22–3 November 1912 that he could promise nothing more than consultation in the event of a threat to the peace of Europe.

However, the fact remained that the *entente* had deeper implications than the government was prepared to admit. The staff talks had begun to gain a momentum of their own. Churchill – as Williamson suggests – would never have taken up the idea of a withdrawal of warships from the Mediterranean so readily had he not believed that the French could actually be relied upon to do what was expected of them. There was an important corollary. It was becoming increasingly difficult for Britain to hold back in a crisis involving France without damage to her international credibility. Nor could the British stop Paris from putting its own interpretation upon what London wished to treat as no more than a 'moral' *entente*. Even this included hints of duty or moral obligation in certain eventualities. Grey himself began to talk of resignation if the cabinet failed to honour the *entente* in a crisis.[27]

Grey was equally determined to preserve the alliance with Japan to ease the calls on the navy. British reductions in the Far East had gone beyond those envisaged in the first years of the alliance. Its renewal in 1911 provoked some criticism (including objections from the Australian government). But Grey protested that non-renewal would have the most serious naval implications. He claimed that without the alliance Britain would need – in order to protect her sea communications to the Far East and between China and Australasia – a separate fleet 'which would be at least equal to a two-Power standard in those waters'. Such a fleet could not be created without yielding naval supremacy to Germany in the North Sea. To end the alliance would also make Japan's future conduct more unpredictable – and the alliance as it was could act only as a possible, rather than a certain restraint on Japan. The latter already possessed eleven capital ships and thirty cruisers. 'In the interests of strategy, in the interests of [limiting] naval expenditure and in the interests of stability', the Japanese alliance had to be renewed.[28]

While Grey's talk of a two-power Far Eastern fleet need not be taken seriously, the commitment would still have been an expensive one. Its implications become evident when note is taken of Churchill's admission to Parliament in 1912 that the British battlefleet was being built against Germany alone, the aim being to preserve a 60 per cent superiority in capital ships. In fact, this decision had been taken in secret as early as 1909. Only shortly before the war in 1914 was there perhaps a hint of future relief for the British naval estimates when the expansion of the French and Russian armies began to force Germany to spend more on her army to counter the growing competition on land.

Among modern historians Zara Steiner has asked why there was 'perpetual talk of an impending war between Britain and Germany when there was nothing concrete to fight over'.[29] Among contemporaries, including Grey's advisers in the Foreign Office, there was some uncertainty as to the seriousness or at least the imminence of the German threat (see Documents 19–21). Balfour was torn between on the one hand his fear of German ambition and ruthlessness, and on the other his amazement that one could talk of conflict in 1912 as 'inevitable' when there was 'no quarrel. . . . . We live in strange times'. But he clung firmly to the belief that Germany would not dare to fight until Britain's naval lead had been reduced.[30]

In practice it was not simply the German navy, but also Berlin's insistence that naval concessions must be dependent upon British neutrality in any war on the Continent which prevented a fundamental improvement in Anglo-German relations. Grey and the Foreign Office (see Document 22) feared that a promise of British neutrality would ultimately expose Britain to the 'combination of the strongest Navy with that of the strongest Army' in the world. With such forces Germany would enjoy 'wider possibilities of influence and action than have yet been possessed by any Empire in Modern Times'.[31]

The British had learned to accommodate themselves to the brute facts of the rise of the United States. In this case, distance and the current modesty of that power's ambitions outside its own continent facilitated a *rapprochement* based upon more than a common language and other forms of kinship. Germany was nearer, and her economic power was being translated into more substantial threats (direct and indirect) to 'perceived British interests'. As Paul Kennedy argues, here was an antagonism which could be removed only if one or the other radically revised its view of its proper place in the world. It was a classic struggle between an upholder and a challenger of the status quo.[32]

At the same time one must be very clear about Britain's place in the power game immediately before the outbreak of war in August 1914. The following propositions will serve as a guide to the ensuing and final section. The Anglo-German antagonism, despite its importance in the international rivalries of the time, was not a direct cause of the outbreak of that war (as opposed to some hypothetical war at a later date). It is also difficult to see how Britain could have prevented that conflict. And finally, Britain could have avoided involvement only through a fundamental revision of the assumptions guiding national policy.

To 1914 – change and continuity

By 1914 British civilian and military leaders, it has been argued, seemed almost as constrained in their choices as their French and German counterparts. Williamson concludes that the Anglo-French military and naval exchanges, while they did not guarantee British involvement in a war, shaped British strategy once the political decision for war was taken in August 1914.[33] Even at the time there were those who questioned whether British policy-makers could not have made wiser choices in the ten or twelve years before 1914. Many historians have subsequently asked whether British foreign policy was sufficiently flexible, imaginative and influential. Some have argued that through an alliance with France and Russia, perhaps backed by a conscript army, Britain might have deterred Germany from war. Others have taken a very different position and have contended that Britain should have played the mediator rather than relied on old balance-of-power policies.[34]

How, then, should British foreign and defence policies in the early twentieth century be appraised? Clearly there had been important changes compared with the previous century. True, the British had suffered several invasion scares in the earlier period. Britain had been active around much of the periphery of Europe, and most consistently in the Near East. Otherwise her interests had been most at risk in other continents. Her influence in the central land mass – France, Germany, Austria and Russia – had been limited at best. But at its lowest this had seemed tolerable (or, in very many cases, welcome) as long as there was no threat to the balance of power comparable to that which existed before 1815 or after 1905.

If Britain had not always had the allies she ideally needed, in practice her foreign and defence policies had mostly been equal to a succession of challenges. At worst, the setbacks had been bearable (such as the concessions to the United States). In other instances time had been bought. There had even been notable (if sometimes only ephemeral) successes. But the overall record had seemed so remarkable that the failure to avoid war in 1914 generated the belief that some fundamental errors must have been committed in or before that year. Surely, many insisted, the British leadership could have done more to prevent the catastrophe, or have been better prepared to meet it. But this is to ignore the degree to which Britain had flourished before 1900 not simply on her merits, but also because of the degree to which the other powers had – for whatever reasons – exercised ultimate restraint or neutralised one another.

Theoretically, in the ten years or so before 1914, the British possessed a number of policy options.

a) The policy of *entente*, backed up by a decisive naval lead over Germany, but with only as large and effective an expeditionary force to assist (perhaps) France and/or Belgium as British politics permitted or interests appeared to dictate. This was the policy which was actually pursued.

b) An alliance with France (and even Russia), possibly backed by the creation of a large military force ready for dispatch at short notice to the Continent.

c) A return to the pre-*entente* policies in the hope that, no matter how the continental powers behaved, Britain would always be able to protect her interests by whatever means seemed appropriate.

d) An imaginative and sustained attempt to play the honest broker in Europe, perhaps backed by the threat to support the weaker party in a crisis.

Defence and diplomacy

e) A policy of isolation and neutrality, on the assumption that British interests would not suffer, or that a loss of influence was preferable to war.

Option (a), the policy of *entente*, was tried; in the sense of preventing war or placing Britain in a strong position in 1914 (other than at sea), it must be accounted a failure. But it is necessary to emphasise that it was treated by the cabinet as a viable choice until very late in the day. The Prime Minister, even on 2 August, could talk of ties with France, not obligations. He conceded that it was in Britain's interest for France to survive as a power, and that Germany should not use the English Channel as 'a hostile base'. But he also insisted that the dispatch of the expeditionary force to Europe was 'out of the question and would serve no object'. While some ministers were clearer in their own minds in favour of war or peace, many could cling to the hope, for instance, that Germany might confine any military intervention in Belgium to the region south of the Meuse. Other uncertainties could be cited to justify the refusal to opt for war at that particular moment.[35] British interests and freedom of action, it seemed, could still be safeguarded by the flexibility provided by option (a).

The alliance option (b) is firmly dismissed by Williamson[36] and others for domestic political reasons. Even Grey could carry the cabinet and Liberal Party no further than the *ententes*. On the Unionist Opposition benches, Balfour ingeniously speculated that an alliance with France might prove acceptable to the British public provided each party agreed that, if attacked, it was willing to submit its case to arbitration.[37] But if, for purposes of argument, one accepts the idea of an alliance as a possibility, it by no means follows that the leaders in Berlin in July–August 1914 would have found this much more intimidating than an *entente*. Only the existence of a conscript British army, ready and able to intervene at short notice on the Continent, might have made a real difference. But having speculated thus far, one must go further and suggest that had such a force been in the process of creation (and this would have taken some years) Berlin would have had an option of its own – namely, that of a pre-emptive strike against France. This would have been theoretically possible at least until Russia could pose a credible military threat to the German frontier in the east.

A return to the 'free hand' option (c) had its attractions even to some in the Foreign Office in the immediate pre-war years. But as we have seen, the *ententes* were designed to control British differences with France and Russia as well as to offer security against Germany. The 'free hand' under Salisbury belonged to an era when no power seemed to have the inclination (even if Germany perhaps had the means) to upset the balance in Europe. Furthermore, Salisbury himself had at one time resorted to the limited expedient of the Mediterranean Agreements. Any pursuit of the 'free hand' in the period before 1914 would also have required more British military strength in the Mediterranean and India. Nevertheless it is interesting to note that in the early months of 1914 some in London did entertain hopes that a more stable environment might be emerging. In April the CID assumed that the international situation was unlikely to change over the next three or four years. France and Russia were coming to be seen as militarily the equal of Germany and Austria-Hungary.[38] But war intervened before any new thinking on policy had time to develop.

The honest broker option (d) would have demanded a formidable British sense of security and self-confidence, as well as a remarkable degree of co-operation and restraint on the part of the other powers. In so far as Grey was able to act as 'honest broker' after the First Balkan War in 1912–13, he was assisted by Russia's relative weakness and German restraint. The episode highlights the limits of British influence – not its strength. The final option of isolation and detachment (e) was unthinkable to almost all those with power and influence in Britain.

If the above conclusions are accepted, it can be argued that while the detail of the foreign and defence policies actually pursued from 1902 may be criticised on various counts, the choice of option (a) was hardly surprising, nor was it an unnatural departure from the variants in policy pursued by Britain towards Europe since 1815. The wisest of the British leadership, even when most confident of Britain's overall strength and security, had always been conscious of the extent to which interests and commitments had run ahead of national and imperial resources, whether assessed in the light of current political constraints or against some hypothetical ideal. To meet this problem the British had had to rely on and exploit the weaknesses, divisions and distractions of others. But in August 1914 the situation was very different. Berlin felt able to risk war with Russia and France and – if necessary – with Britain. Even if the British cabinet as a whole had awoken to the dangers of all-out war

115

earlier than they did, it is doubtful whether the outcome would have been different.[39]

As it was, many ministers seemed to be thinking themselves back to the outbreak of the Franco-Prussian War in 1870. It was the new information and developments from 2 August which changed their minds. The Prime Minister learned that the Unionists were eager to support France and Russia. From Paris came promises to respect Belgian neutrality, whereas Berlin sent the notorious ultimatum to Brussels. Asquith began to ask questions about French vulnerability and the value of the British expeditionary force on the Continent. Once Belgium as a whole was seen to be under threat, the mood in Britain changed markedly in favour of war. Michael Brock makes two very important points. He notes that it is 'highly probable' that even if there had been no serious fighting in Belgium, the British would still – in due course – have joined the war beside the French armies. But without Belgium they would have gone to war as a divided people, at a later time, and after a great ministerial crisis.[40]

Belgium thus did what key British diplomats and strategists could not do despite all their recourse to the logic of power politics – a logic which went as far as to claim that Britain had to fight to ensure not only that German ambitions were defeated, but also that Russia and France did not win without her. They were arguing that Britain had to contribute to the victory if she was to be sufficiently influential in the post-war environment (similar arguments were to have a great effect on an American President in 1917). British entry into the war on 4 August still meant that the main brunt of the fighting on land was borne initially by others. In time the British surprised even themselves with the scale of their war effort. American loans, however, were of increasing importance even before the United States entered the war in 1917. In the end it was the transatlantic power which tipped the balance and which in the course of 1918 came to occupy a position bearing a number of resemblances to that enjoyed by Britain in 1814–15.

Notes

1 Mackay, *Balfour*, pp. 115–16.

2 J. Holland Rose, *Cambridge History of the British Empire*, Cambridge, 1929–59, iii. 567.

3 Spiers, *Haldane*, p. 2; Mackay, *Balfour*, p. 117. For the army before and during the Boer War see E. M. Spiers, *The Late Victorian Army, 1868–1902*, Manchester, 1992.

4 Mackay, *Balfour*, pp. 122, 126; Beckett and Gooch, *Politicians*, p. 71; Spiers, *Haldane*, pp. 188–9.

5 D. G. Boyce (ed.), *The Crisis of British Power; the imperial and naval papers of the second Earl of Selborne, 1895–1919*, London, 1990, pp. 106, 115. See Friedberg, *Weary Titan*, pp. 172–3.

6 Bourne, *Foreign Policy*, p. 472.

7 Greaves, *Persia*, pp. 192, 214, Boyce, *Selborne*, p. 155.

8 R. Williams, *Defending the Empire*, New Haven and London, 1991, p. 23. See also C. Barnett, *Britain and her Army, 1509–1970*, London, 1970, p. 274; M. Beloff, *Britain's Liberal Empire, 1897–1921*, London, 1969, p. 37.

9 For the debates on the defence of India, note G. W. Monger, *The End of Isolation; British foreign policy 1900–7*, London, 1963, pp. 147, 172–3; Boyce, *Selborne*, pp. 155, 163–7; Greaves, *Persia*, pp. 15–17, 221–2; Friedberg, *Weary Titan*, pp. 217, 249–51, 260; Mackay, *Balfour*, pp. 157–9.

10 For Britain and the German navy, see Friedberg, *Weary Titan*, pp. 190, 203–7, 266–9; Boyce, *Selborne*, pp. 142, 171; A. J. Marder, *From Dreadnought to Scapa Flow*, London, 1961, i. 472–3; R. F. Mackay, 'The Admiralty, the German navy, and the redistribution of the British Fleet, 1904–5'. *The Mariner's Mirror*, LVI, 1970, pp. 341–6. Mackay notes the influence of the Russo-Japanese War on British planning. The French fleet was described as standing in 'the forefront', with the German threat as a potential rather than an immediate one.

11 P. M. Kennedy, *The Realities behind Diplomacy: background influences on British external policy, 1865–1980*, London, 1981, p. 125.

12 S. R. Williamson, *The Politics of Grand Strategy: Britain and France prepare for war, 1904–14*, Cambridge, Mass., 1969, pp. 44 ff.

13 *Ibid.*, pp. 61 ff., 84.

14 *Ibid.*, p. 278.

15 Spiers, *Haldane*, p. 188.

16 *Ibid*, p. 199.

17 For army reform and planning, see *ibid.*, pp. 73, 77–83, 154–60, 175–81, 185–6.

18 Williamson, *Grand Strategy*, pp. 108 ff.; C. J. Lowe and M. L. Dockrill, *The Mirage of Power; British foreign policy, 1902–22*, London, 1972, ii. 441–5.

19 Williamson, *Grand Strategy*, pp. 108–14, 132.

20 *Ibid.*, pp. 139–41, 151–3.

21 *Ibid.*, pp. 370–1.

22   Lowe, *Mirage*, ii. 445–6; Spiers, *Haldane*, p. 192.

23   Williamson, *Grand Strategy*, pp. 191–5.

24   *Ibid.*, pp. 199–204.

25   Kennedy, *Naval Mastery*, p. 291. For the Anglo-German naval race see Marder, *Dreadnought*, *passim*.

26   Kennedy, *Naval Mastery*, pp. 223–5.

27   Williamson, *Grand Strategy*, pp. 284–99.

28   Kennedy, *Naval Mastery*, p. 221; compare with Friedberg's critique in *Weary Titan*, pp. 299–300 that Britain should have acted on her own in the Far East.

29   Z. Steiner, *Britain and the Origins of the First World War*, London and Basingstoke, 1977, p. 42.

30   Mackay, *Balfour*, p. 242.

31   Steiner, *Origins*, p. 42.

32   P. M. Kennedy, *The Rise of the Anglo-German Anatagonism, 1860– 1914*, London, 1980, pp. 466, 470.

33   Williamson, *Grand Strategy*, pp. 371–2.

34   C. J. Bartlett, *British Foreign Policy in the Twentieth Century*, London, 1989, pp. 20–3.

35   R. J. W. Evans and H. P. von Strandmann (eds.), *The Coming of the First World War*, Oxford, pp. 145–52.

36   Williamson, *Grand Strategy*, pp. 368 ff.

37   Mackay, *Balfour*, p. 243.

38   Evans and von Strandmann, pp. 147, 163–4.

39   See, for example, John W. Langdon, *July 1914: the long debate, 1918–90*, New York and Oxford, 1991, pp. 120–1, 127–9, 153–4, 179–80 for various views on the course of events in July 1914.

40   Evans and von Strandmann, pp. 174–5, and see chapter 7, *passim*.

Selected documents

The extracts from documents in the Public Record Office (London) are reproduced with the permission of the Controller of Her Majesty's Stationery Office.

Document 1

A cabinet memorandum of 26 December 1813 outlined ministerial ideas on a suitable peace settlement (Public Record Office, London, FO 139/1). See H. W. V. Temperley, and L. M. Penson, *Foundations of British Foreign Policy from Pitt to Salisbury* (Cambridge, 1938), pp. 29–34.

> ... the objects *sine Qua Non* upon which G[rea]t Britain can venture to divest herself of her [colonial] Conquests in any material degree are, 1st the Absolute Exclusion of France from any Naval Establishment on the Scheldt, and Especially at Antwerp and 2ndly The Security of Holland being adequately provided for ...
>
> It must also be understood that the Monarchies of the Peninsula must also be Independent under their Legitimate Sovereigns. Their Dominions at least in Europe being guaranteed against attack by France....
>
> Malta being Always understood to Remain British ...
>
> The Mauritius is retained as being when in the hands of an Enemy a most Injurious Station to our Indian Commerce ...
>
> The Cape of Good Hope is excepted [among the colonies to be returned to the Dutch], as a Position connected with the Security of our Empire in the East ...

The Treaty of Alliance not to terminate with the War, but to Contain defensive Engagements with eventual obligations to support the Powers attack'd by France, with a certain extent of Stipulated Succours.

Document 2

Castlereagh's hopes concerning great-power co-operation were set out in his circular dispatch of 1 January 1816 (PRO: FO 143 France 12), See C. K. Webster, *The Foreign Policy of Castlereagh, 1815–22* (London, 1925), pp. 509–12.

You must not however suppose that I counsel you to become the dupe of designing men . . . but I wish you without running into such an extreme to inspire as far as possible a temper of morality and confidence amongst those who are accredited to the same Court. The language of such a Power as Great Britain is calculated in itself to do much; but when its views are understood, when it is distinctly known to be leagued with no particular Court to the oppression of another, that its only object is the peace of the world, and that it is determined to use all its means to combine the Powers of Europe against that State whose perverted policy or criminal ambition shall first menace the repose in which all have a common interest – I am sanguine in my hopes that the most salutary results may be expected from such a line of policy.

Document 3

The Admiralty's views on future naval strength were reported by the Secretary of the Admiralty to the Navy Board on 8 December 1815 (PRO: Admiralty 2/1382 fos, 281–6). See C. J. Bartlett, *Great Britain and Sea Power, 1815–53* (Oxford, 1963), pp. 23–4.

My Lords Commissioners of the Admiralty feel it to be their duty to take at this juncture a general view of the state of the ships of His Majesty's Navy with the purpose of making all the reduction of expense in time of peace which may be consistent with an adequate preparation for the event of war.

The first object of their Lordships' attention is the force which it may be proper to keep in a state of readiness for sea and actual service. This force, my Lords are of opinion, should be about one hundred sail of the line (exclusive of ships building) fourteen of which are to be in commission as Guard and Flag ships; and the others should be laid up in ordinary in such a state of repair and equipment as will admit of their being on any emergency brought forward for immediate service. . . .

These observations with regard to Ships of the Line apply in good measure to fourth and fifth rates [ie frigates], of which my Lords think an effective number of one hundred and sixty, including 4 fourth rates, and 26 fifth rates in commission, will be sufficient to answer all the probable demands of the publick service.

(Note also the The Select Parliamentary Committee on Finance in 1817–18 argued that 'the Naval Superiority of this Country . . . [is] the principle on which its external power, internal safety, and general prosperity, in the highest degree depend . . . there is no part of the Public Service in which an ill-judged temporary economy might be ultimately productive of such considerable expense.' See Bartlett, p. 21.)

Document 4

Cabinet divisions over the recognition of Spain's former Latin American colonies prompted the writing of the following memorandum in November–December 1824. The authorship is uncertain, but it expresses the views of Liverpool and Canning, See C. D. Yonge, *The Life and Administration of Robert Banks, Earl of Liverpool* (London, 1868), iii. 297–304. This is also cited by H. W. V. Temperley, *The Foreign Policy of Canning, 1822–27* (London, 1925), pp. 550–5.

The great and favourite object of the policy of this country, for more than four centuries, has been to foster and encourage our navigation, as the sure basis of our maritime power. In this branch of national industry the people of the United States are become more formidable rivals to us than any other nation which has ever yet existed. . . .

Let us recollect that, as their commercial marine is augmented, their military marine must proportionately increase. And it cannot be doubted that, if we provoke the new states of [Spanish] America tc give a decided preference in their ports to the people of the United States over ourselves, the navigation of these extensive dominions will be lost to us, and it will, in a great measure, be transferred to our rivals.

Let us remember, then, that peace, however desirable, and however cherished by us, cannot last for ever. Sooner or later we shall probably have to contend with the combined maritime power of France and of the United States. The disposition of the new States is at present highly favourable to England. If we take advantage of that disposition, we may establish through our influence with them a fair counterpoise to that combined maritime power.

Document 5

Wellington's thinking on foreign policy is revealingly set out in this letter to Sir Herbert Taylor in December 1824. See Wellington, Duke of, ed., *Dispatches, Correspondence and Memoranda of the Duke of Wellington* (London, 1867–80), ii. 381–3.

There is nothing so necessary as to look forward to future wars, and to our early preparation for them. Our wars have always been long and ruinous in expense, because we were unable to prepare for the operations which must have brought them to a close, for years after they were commenced. But this system will no longer answer. We cannot venture upon any great augmentation of our debt, if we did we should find the payment of the interest impossible, together with the expense of our peace establishments. We must, therefore, take great care to keep ourselves out of disputes if possible, and above all, to keep our neighbours quiet; and next to put our resources for war on such a footing as that we may apply them hereafter at a much earlier period of the contest than we have ever done hitherto.

Document 6

Palmerston justified his stand against Russia, Austria and Prussia to Lord Melbourne on 1 March 1836. See L. C. Sanders, ed., *Lord Melbourne Papers* (London, 1890), pp. 337–40. Extracts are cited by K. Bourne, *The Foreign Policy of Victorian Britain, 1830–1902* (Oxford, 1972), pp. 226–8.

... The division of Europe into two camps ... is the result of events beyond our control, and is the consequence of the French Revolution of July [1830] ... The separation is not one of words but of things; not the effect of caprice or will, but produced by the force of occurrences. The three [Russia, Austria and Prussia] and the two [Britain and France] think differently, and therefore they

act differently, whether it be as to Belgium, or Portugal, or Spain. . . .
The plain English of it all is, that they [Russia, Austria and Prussia]
want to have England on their side against France, that they may
dictate to France as they did in 1814 and 1815; and they are
provoked beyond measure at the steady protection which France
has derived from us. But it is the protection which has preserved
the peace of Europe . . .

Document 7

Palmerston strongly defended his Near Eastern policy on 5 July
1840 to the Prime Minister. See H. L. Bulwer, *The Life of Henry John
Temple, Viscount Palmerston* (London, 1870), ii. 356–61. See also
Bourne, pp. 243–6.

My opinion upon this question is distinct and unqualified. I think
that the object to be attained is of the utmost importance for the
interests of England, for the preservation of the balance of power,
and for the maintenance of peace in Europe. I find the three
Powers [Russia, Austria and Prussia] entirely prepared to concur
in the views which I entertain on this matter. . . .

The immediate result of our declining to go on with the three
Powers because France does not join us will be, that Russia will
withdraw her offers to unite herself with the other Powers for
a settlement of the affairs of Turkey, and she will again resume
her separate and isolated position with respect to those affairs;
and you will have the treaty of Unkiar Skelessi renewed under
some still more objectionable form . . . and England will, by her
own voluntary and deliberate act, re-establish the separate
protectorship of Russia over Turkey . . .

The ultimate results of such a division will be the practical
division of Turkey into two separate and independent states,
whereof one [Egypt] will be the dependency of France, and the
other a satellite of Russia; and in both of which our political influence will be sacrificed; and this dismemberment will inevitably
give rise to local struggles and conflicts which will involve the
Powers of Europe in most serious disputes.

Document 8

Palmerston's readiness to take risks in 1840 alarmed the Admiralty
and many naval officers given the current (if temporary) weaknesses of the British Mediterranean squadron. The views of one

were quoted by C. M. McHardy. 'The British navy for one hundred years', *The Navy League Journal*, March 1896, p. 3 (see Bartlett, p. 139).

> In 1840 (at which period I commanded the *Thunderer* in the Mediterranean), the different Captains on that station were in the month of August officially warned that we might expect shortly to come into hostile collision with the French Fleet. At that period our ships were on peace establishments and even then we were short of complement . . .
>
> The first reinforcement of seamen, or rather persons so called, did not arrive until the month of January (six months after the warning was given) and it amounted to 600 men only.
>
> Thus we were left for a period of six months expecting continually . . . to come into collision with the French fleet, the ships composing which were fully manned, and no means spared to render them in every respect efficient.

Document 9

Palmerston on 9 August 1847 outlined Britain's strategic needs in Western Europe when there was talk of a possible union of Spain and Portugal. See E. Ashley, *The Life of Henry John Temple, Viscount Palmerston: 1846–65* (London, 1877), i. 18–20. Extracts are cited by Bourne, pp. 275–7.

> . . . the naval position of the Tagus ought never to be in the hands of any power, whether French or Spanish, which might become hostile to England, and it is only by maintaining Portugal in its separate existence, and in its intimate and protected state of alliance with England, that we can be sure of having the Tagus as a friendly . . . naval station. Only fancy for a moment Portugal forming part of Spain, and Spain led away by France into war with England, and what would be our condition with all the ports from Calais to Marseilles hostile to us . . . and with nothing between us and Malta but Gibraltar, the capture of which would be the bait which France would hold out to Spain to induce her to go to war with us.

Document 10

Lord John Russell's memorandum of 10 January 1848 is a good example of the early fears of the effects of steamships on British

security. See S. Walpole, *The Life of Lord John Russell* (London, 1889),
ii. 18–23, cited in part by Bartlett, pp. 190–1. (Note also a letter on
this subject by Wellington published in the press in 1847, and
printed by George Wrottesley, *Life and Correspondence of Sir John
Burgoyne* (London, 1873), i. 444–51. The crucial sections are cited by
M. J. Salvoulis, *"Riflemen Form": the war scare of 1859–60 in England*
(London and New York, 1982), p. 10.)

> [Russell wrote] It can hardly be doubted that the French have for a
> long time made preparations for a naval war; that such pre-
> parations can be directed against no other power than England;
> and that the preparations of England have been, as usual in such
> cases, slackened by the security which the great victories of the end
> of the last war have inspired.
> There are three modes by which the French may injure and
> assail England on the breaking out of a war:
> 1. By sending steamers to alarm our coasts and interrupt our
> trade as proposed by the Prince de Joinville.
> 2. By landing a force to bombard and destroy our naval and
> military arsenals.
> 3. By invading England with an army of 30,000 or 40,000 men,
> and marching at once on London.

Document 11

Palmerston put the case for a pragmatic and flexible foreign policy
to the House of Commons on 1 March 1848. Russia, France (irrespective of the regime in power) and even Austria were all possible
partners. Hansard 3rd series, xcvii, 121–3. See also Bourne, pp.
291–3.

> I hold with respect to alliances that, England is a power sufficiently
> strong, sufficiently powerful, to steer her own course, and not to
> tie herself as an unnecessary appendage to the policy of any other
> Government. . . . and as long as she sympathises with right and
> justice, she never will find herself altogether alone. She is sure to
> find some other State, of sufficient power, influence, and weight, to
> support and aid her in the course she may think fit to pursue.
> Therefore I say that it is a narrow policy to suppose that this
> country or that is to be marked out as the eternal ally or the
> perpetual enemy of England. We have no eternal allies, and we
> have no perpetual enemies. Our interests are eternal and
> perpetual.

Document 12

Lord Panmure, soon after his appointment as Secretary of State for War, wrote at length in February 1855 on the need for military re-organisation in response to the mounting alarm over the state of the army in the Crimea. See Sir George Douglas and Sir George Dalhousie Ramsay, eds., *The Panmure Papers* (London, 1908), i. 46–51.

... the people of this country have always been in the habit of looking to their insular position as a reason why they should depend more on a navy than an army for their protection, and have looked to the former only as necessary to afford protection to our colonies, and to maintain order and respect for the law at home [save in time of a great war].

They have never looked on the Army as a force which was to be kept available for foreign aggression.

... every Ministry for the last forty years has striven, one after another, who shall gain most popularity by reducing our Army to the lowest possible amount with which the colonial reliefs could be carried on without subjecting our soldiers to absolute exile from their native country.

... I trust our present experience will prove to our countrymen that our Army must be something more than a mere colonial guard or home police; that it must be the means of maintaining our name abroad, and causing it to be respected in peace as well as admired and dreaded in war. ...

I concur in HRH's [the Prince Consort's] remarks that our Army is 'a mere aggregate of battalions' – each of these perfect in itself and admirably formed, governed, and drilled, but only pieces in the entire structure of an army, as the wheels, etc., are in the mechanism of a clock.

... The system by which an army should be provisioned, moved, brought to act in the field and in the trenches, taught to attack or defend, is non-existent. ...

We have no means of making General Officers or of forming an efficient Staff, as it has been the practice ... to keep the same officers constantly in employment, till they have either become worn out, or so wedded to old ways as to be useless when called to the field. ...

... I come now to our force in time of peace. This should never be under 100,000 bayonets, of which 25,000 will probably be in India, 12,000 should be in Gibraltar and the Mediterranean ... leaving 63,000 for home service and the colonies. ... [The colonial needs] would reduce the home force to 51,500. Of these, three

divisions of 10,000 each should be formed to be placed in permannent cantonments and occasionally encamped in such localities in
England, Scotland and Ireland as afford sufficient space for training and exercise, and easy access by railway. . . .

All [the reforms] that I have pointed out may be achieved under
even the present system of command, but I would be wanting in
candour did I not state my opinion, that I believe it can only be
done by vesting in a Minister of the Crown the control and
responsibility for the co-operation of all the branches of the Military Service.

Document 13

Palmerston between 1859 and '65 worked both to conciliate France
and to demonstrate to her government the dangers of war with
Britain. In a private letter of 8 January 1865 he set out the fundamentals of his policies over the years. See Temperley and Penson,
pp. 293–4.

> The standing Policy of France is to make the Mediterranean a
> French Lake, and they steadily pursue it on every favourable
> occasion. If we maintain our Superiority at Sea . . . we should prob
> ably be able, in the Event of war to drive them out of most of the
> Positions they might acquire . . . Prevention is better than Cure.
> Our Business consequently ought to be to unravel their Plots, to
> see through their Intrigues, and to defeat their schemes by
> Counteraction steadily and Systematically applied . . . They also
> know, and have learnt by experience, that when England and
> France are at variance Austria, Russia and Prussia are much more
> disposed to join with us than with France, and what the French
> wish most to avoid is a European Coalition against them.

Document 14

One of Salisbury's first acts as Foreign Secretary was to draft his
famous circular dispatch of I April 1878 on the Near Eastern crisis
and in response to the Treaty of San Stefano (PRO: FO 244/314;
Parliamentary Papers, 1878, lxxxi, 756–72) [c1989]). See Temperley
and Penson, pp. 372–80, and (extracts) Bourne, pp. 412–13.

> . . . The general effect of this portion of the Treaty [permitting some
> Russian influence in Thessaly and Epirus] will be to increase the
> power of the Russian Empire in the countries where a Greek

population predominates, not only to the prejudice of the nation
[Turkey], but also of every country having interests in the east of
the Mediterranean Sea. . . .

. . . Their [the terms of the treaty's] combined effect, in addition
to the results . . . upon the balance of maritime power . . . is to
depress, almost to the point of entire subjection, the political independence of the Government of Constantinople. The formal jurisdiction of that Government extends over geographical positions
which must, under all circumstances, be of the deepest interest to
Great Britain. It is in the power of the Ottoman Government to
close or to open the Straits which form the natural highway of
nations between the Aegean Sea and the Euxine. Its dominion is
recognized at the head of the Persian Gulf, on the shores of the
Levant, and in the immediate neighbourhood of the Suez Canal. It
cannot be otherwise than a matter of extreme solicitude to this
country that the Government to which this jurisdiction belongs
should be so closely pressed by the political outposts of a greatly
superior Power that its independent action, and even existence, is
almost impossible. . . . A discussion limited to Articles selected by
one Power in the Congress would be an illusory remedy for the
dangers to English interests and to the permanent peace of Europe,
which would result from the state of things which the Treaty
proposes to establish.

Salisbury added in a private letter to his ambassador in Constantinople of 9 May 1878 (Temperley and Penson, pp. 384–5; Bourne,
pp. 413–14):

And, while Russian influence over the provinces of European
Turkey would be a comparatively distant and indirect evil, her
influence over Syria and Mesopotamia would be a very serious
embarrassment, and would certainly through the connection of
Bagdad with Bombay, make our hold on India more difficult.

Document 15

The keen debate in the mid-1890s on British interests in the future
of the Ottoman Empire prompted an emphatic statement of British
needs by the Director of Naval Intelligence, 28 October 1896 (PRO:
Adm. 116/866B), cited by Bourne, pp. 446–9. (See also the views
of the Director of Military Intelligence of 13 October 1896 in
A. J. Marder, *The Anatomy of British Sea Power, 1880–1905* (London,
1964), pp. 569 ff.)

(1) The Sultan of Turkey is antagonistic to England and friendly to Russia – therefore the assistance of the Turks cannot now be counted on by us against Russia.

(2) The established friendship of France and Russia puts it beyond doubt that in war with either we should have to reckon with both. . . .

. . . If the course of time is to see Russia in Asia Minor with a naval base in the Eastern basin of the Mediterranean, France still in alliance with her, or herself established in Syria, there would be only one way in which England could not only maintain herself in the Mediterranean at all, but to continue to hold India, and that is by holding Egypt against all comers and making Alexandria into a naval base.

. . . Europe [can be defied] if Egypt is strongly held and Alexandria, Malta and Gibraltar are naval bases. This is England's policy of the future, to work for this end should be her aim – do nothing that can jeopardise it, but quietly mould events to accomplish it.

. . . Count, that as long as France and Russia act together, England must prepare to meet the Black Sea Fleet in the Mediterranean. Decide, that when a Russian naval base is commenced in Asia, an English naval base must be created in the eastern basin of the Mediterranean, preferably Alexandria. Try to secure that Italy shall guard her own waters . . . Try to secure the good will of Spain and maintain the status quo on the Morocco coast. In a war with France, take Tangier and hold it for Spain to secure her benevolent neutrality.

Document 16

Salisbury summed up his views on the possibility of British inclusion in the Triple Alliance of Germany, Austria-Hungary and Italy on 29 May 1901 (PRO: Cab 37/57 no. 52). See G. P. Gooch and H. Temperley, *British Documents on the Origins of the War, 1898–1914* (HMSO, 1926–38), ii. 68–9, and Bourne, pp. 462–4.

. . . The liability of having to defend the German and Austrian frontiers against Russia is heavier than *having to defend the British Isles against France*. Even, therefore, in its most naked aspect the bargain would be a bad one for the country. Count Hatzfeldt speaks of our *'isolation'* as constituting a serious danger for us. *Have we ever felt that danger practically?* If we had succumbed in the revolutionary war, our fall would not have been due to our isolation. We had many allies, but they would not have saved us if the French Emperor had been able to command the Channel. Except during his reign we have never even been in danger; and, therefore, it is impossible for us to judge whether the 'isolation' under which we are supposed to suffer, does or does not contain in it any elements of peril. It would be hardly wise to incur novel and most onerous obligations, in order to guard against *a danger in whose existence we have no historical reason for believing.*

Document 17

Lord Lansdowne summed up British worries over the future of Persia in a letter of 6 January 1902 (FO Persia 649 no. 2). See Gooch and Temperley, iv. 369–70.

The Persian Government must be well aware, from the experience of 100 years, that Great Britain has no designs upon the sovereignty of the Shah or the independence of his State. It has, on the contrary, been one of our principal objects to encourage and strengthen the States lying outside the frontier of our Indian Empire, with the hope that we should find in them an intervening zone sufficient to prevent direct contact between the dominions of Great Britain and those of other great military Powers. . . .

The Persian Government should . . . distinctly understand . . . that Great Britain could not consent to the acquisition by Russia of a military or naval station in the Persian Gulf, for the reason that such a station must be regarded as a challenge to Great Britain and a menace to her Indian Empire. . . .

Nor, again, could His Majesty's government acquiesce in the concession to Russia of any preferential political rights or advantages, or any commercial monopoly or exclusive privilege in the southern or south-eastern districts of Persia.

The Committee of Imperial Defence agreed on 22 March 1903 (iv. 371):

1. It is essential to maintain, and if possible to increase, our influence in Tehran, in order that we may be able to control railway construction in Persia, which is by far the most important factor in the strategic situation, and also for commercial reasons.

2. It should be our object, on commercial as well as on strategic grounds, to maintain the *status quo* in Persia.

3. It is essential to maintain our existing claims on the coast of the Persian Gulf without aggression or ostentation.

Document 18

The General Staff highlighted the difficulties of war with Russia in their comments on the proposed renewal of the Anglo-Japanese Alliance on 16 June 1905 (FO Japan 673, no. 101). See Gooch and Temperley, iv. 137–40.

> . . . Japan might, however, expect us to take military measures against Russia in other parts of the world, and this, with the possible exception of taking advantage of such insurrectionary movements as at present obtain in the Caucasus, we could only do through Afghanistan. . . .
>
> In the event of France or Germany being hostile . . . the first and main attack by these Powers would be made in the Western Hemisphere, and the brunt of it we should have to bear unaided. Regarded from this standpoint, Japan – a very shrewd nation – would appear to have decidedly the best of the bargain. . . .
>
> *Minute:* It is rather surprising to me that this extremely important expression of opinion should not have been elicited earlier in the day by the S[ecretary of] S[tate] for War. . . . L[ansdowne]

Document 19

The German question was examined within the general context of British foreign policy by Eyre Crowe in his classic memorandum of 1 January 1907 (PRO: FO 371/257). See Gooch and Temperley, iii. 397–420, and Bourne, pp. 481–93.

> The general character of England's foreign policy is determined by the immutable conditions of her geographical position on the ocean flank of Europe as an island State with vast overseas colonies and dependencies, whose existence and survival as an independent community are inseparably bound up with the possession of preponderant sea power. . . . Its formidable character makes itself felt the more directly that a maritime State is, in the literal sense of the word, the neighbour of every country accessible by sea. It would, therefore, be but natural that the power of a State supreme at sea should inspire universal jealousy and fear, and be ever exposed to the danger of being overthrown by a general combination of the world. . . . The danger can in practice only be averted . . . on condition that the national policy . . . is closely identified with the primary and vital interests of a majority, or as many as possible, of the other nations. . . .

... The equilibrium established by such a grouping of forces [against a state seeking or enjoying predominance] is technically known as the balance of power, and it has become almost an historical truism to identify England's secular policy with the maintenance of this balance. . . .

By applying this general law to a particular case, the attempt might be made to ascertain whether . . . Germany is, in fact, aiming at a political hegemony . . . and establishing a German primacy in the world of international politics at the cost to and detriment of other nations. . . .

There follows a lengthy discussion of German policy and conduct which, though pessimistic and critical in most respects, does not wholly despair of a satisfactory outcome. He also anticipates a recurrent theme of several British diplomats down to 1914 – that Russia and France, despite the *ententes* – might once again threaten British interests. Crowe continued:

So long as England remains faithful to the general principle of the preservation of the balance of power, her interests would not be served by Germany being reduced to the rank of a weak Power, as this might easily lead to a Franco-Russian predominance equally, if not more, formidable to the British Empire. There are no existing German rights, territorial or other, which this country could wish to see diminished. . . .

. . . there is an impression that Germany will think twice before she now gives rise to any fresh disagreement. In this attitude she will be encouraged if she meets on England's part with unvarying courtesy and consideration in all matters of common concern, but also with a prompt and firm refusal to enter into any one-sided bargains or arrangements. . . .

Document 20

The Permanent Under-Secretary of State for Foreign Affairs, Sir Charles Hardinge, analysed the Anglo-German naval issue on 25 August 1909. See Gooch and Temperley, vi. 285–6.

The cause of the cool relations between England and Germany is the suspicion aroused by the German Naval Programme . . . during the past nine years . . . more especially as there are no pending questions of any importance between the two Gov[ernmen]ts such

as existed with the French and Russian Gov[ernmen]ts at the time
of the conclusion of the Anglo-French and Anglo-Russian agreements. The conclusion of a naval agreement is in reality the only
condition that is needed to ensure more friendly feelings between the Gov[ernmen]ts and people of the two countries. . . .

The issue had prompted Foreign Office minutes on 20 July 1909
(see Gooch and Temperley, vi. 279) to the effect that:

> But still however pacific the German Emperor and German nation
> may be at present the danger lies in the fact of their possessing a
> Navy strong enough to enable them to go in for a warlike policy at
> any moment, when they may feel less pacific. There is a risk that
> when they have got their big fleet they will be strongly tempted to
> try to make somebody else pay for it.

Grey added:

> Yes: and it is natural that till they have a big navy they should
> quiet apprehensions.

Document 21

On 10 November 1909 Harding minuted with respect to German
policy (PRO: FO 40904/31695/09/18). See Gooch and Temperley,
vi. 311–12.

> [Berlin proposed that] a Convention should be made by which the
> two Powers should bind themselves for a fixed period: –
> 1. Not to make war against each other.
> 2. To join in no coalition against either Power and
> 3. To observe a benevolent neutrality should either country be
> engaged in hostilities with any other Power or Powers.
> Were His Majesty's Government to fall into a trap of this kind,
> the duration of the agreement would be strenuously employed by
> Germany to consolidate her supremacy in Europe, while England
> would remain a spectator with her hands tied. At the termination
> of the agreement, Germany would be free to devote her whole
> strength to reducing the only remaining independent factor in
> Europe [England] . . . Moreover the mere announcement that Eng-
> land had concluded such an agreement with Germany would
> result in her immediate isolation, and would entail a loss of pres-
> tige and of any confidence for the future in her loyalty and friend-
> ship.

Document 22

Negotiations with Germany in 1912 alarmed the influential Foreign Official, Eyre Crowe. He feared that Britain might injure her relations with her *entente* partners without gaining any additional security in relation to Germany. Minute of 6 April 1912 (PRO: FO 14431/5569/12/18), cited in Gooch and Temperley, vi. 738–9.

> ... [During the Agadir crisis of 1911] H[is] M[ajesty's] G [overnment] considered that the continued existence of a strong and independent France was of vital interest to this country, and the proposition is too well-founded and too well understood to require to be laboured. Hence HMG intimated that England would stand by France in any quarrel which Germany might endeavour to fasten upon her as arising out of the then situation. . . .
>
> What view have HMG formed of what German policy is? . . . The evidence which is in the possession of this office can leave very little doubt as to what Germany's policy is: She wants to have an absolutely free hand in dealing with any problem of foreign policy without fear of meeting with the opposition of third parties. She wants to make herself so strong that she can dictate terms to every Power. . . . She will leave no stone unturned to drive apart if possible the Powers of the Dual Alliance and England, America, and Japan.

Grey minuted:

> All this is true and not to be disregarded but on the other hand it has to be borne in mind that Russia and France both deal separately with Germany and that it is not unreasonable that tension should be permanently greater between England and Germany that between Germany and France or Germany and Russia.

Sir Arthur Nicolson (Permanent Under-Secretary) went further on 15 April 1912, Gooch and Temperly, vi. 747:

> . . . it would be far more dangerous to have an unfriendly France and Russia than an unfriendly Germany. The latter . . . can give us plenty of annoyance, but it cannot really threaten any of our more important interests, while Russia especially could cause us extreme embarrassment, and, indeed, danger in the Mid-East and on our Indian frontier. . . .

Document 23

A General Staff memorandum of 13 August 1911 not only provided
a mature explanation of Military thinking, but to a remarkable
degree anticipated the strategic justification for British entry into
the First World War (Cab 38/19/47). See C. J. Lowe and M. L.
Dockrill, *The Mirage of Power: British foreign policy, 1902–22* (London
and Boston, 1972), iii. 445–8.

> In this paper it has been assumed that the policy of England is to
> prevent any one or more continental Powers from attaining a
> position of superiority which would enable it or them to dominate
> the other Continental Powers. Such domination . . . would menace
> the independence of the United Kingdom and the integrity of the
> British Empire. . . .
>
> In the case of our remaining neutral, Germany will fight France
> single-handed. The armies of Germany and the fleets of Germany
> are much stronger than those of France, and the results of such a
> war can scarcely be doubted . . . France would in all probability be
> defeated [even with Russian intervention], Holland and Belgium
> might be annexed by Germany. . . .
>
> It seems . . . that in a war between Germany and France in which
> England takes an active part the result in the opening moves might
> be doubtful, but the longer the war lasted the greater the strain
> would be on Germany. . . .
>
> . . . if we once allow Germany to defeat France, our expeditionary
> force would be valueless and the duration of our naval predomin-
> ance could be measured in years.

The memorandum concluded that the expeditionary force should
be sent to France to participate in the 'opening actions', while the
navy covered the movement across the Channel, and defended
Britain from invasion.

Bibliographical Essay

Muriel E. Chamberlain provides an excellent and concise study, *'Pax Britannica'?: British foreign policy, 1789–1914*, London, 1988. Among other works Kenneth Bourne's *The Foreign Policy of Victorian England, 1830–1902*, Oxford, 1970, contains a perceptive and detailed examination of key issues, while the years beyond are well covered by C. J. Lowe and M. L. Dockrill, *The Mirage of Power: British foreign policy, 1902–14*, London, 1972. Students wishing to look at extensive documentation on British foreign policy should consult Bourne, pp. 197 ff, and volume iii of Lowe and Dockrill. There is also the classic introduction to primary material by H. W. V. Temperley and L. M. Penson, *Foundations of British Foreign Policy 1792–1902*, London, 1938.

Defence issues are admirably introduced by David French, *The British Way of Warfare, 1688–2000*, London, 1990; P. M. Kennedy, *The Rise and Fall of British Naval Mastery*, London, 1983; and C. Barnett, *Britain and her Army, 1509–1970*, London, 1970. Defence policy-making is analysed in depth by M. S. Partridge, *Military Planning for the Defense of the United Kingdom, 1814–1870*, New York and London, 1989; J. Gooch, *The Prospect of War: studies in British defence policy, 1847–1942*, London, 1981; D. A. Johnson, *Defence by Committee*, London, 1960; R. F. Mackay, *Balfour: intellectual statesman*, Oxford, 1985; S. R. Williamson, *The Politics of Grand Strategy: Britain and France prepare for war, 1904–14*, Cambridge, Mass., 1969.

W. C. B. Tunstall provides useful surveys of imperial defence in his chapters in *The Cambridge History of the British Empire* (edited by J. Holland Rose, A. P. Newton and E. A. Benians), vols. ii and iii,

Cambridge, 1940 and 1959, Aaron L. Friedberg, *The Weary Titan: Britain and the experience of relative decline, 1895–1905*, Princeton, 1988, offers an interesting study of the interaction between economics and foreign, imperial and defence policies. P. Hopkirk in *The Great Game: on secret service in High Asia*, Oxford, 1991, covers a narrower subject over a longer period, and analyses the interplay between those in the front line and the varied institutions and interests engaged in the defence of India and rivalry with Russia.

For more detailed study of the navy and its role, see C. J. Bartlett, *Great Britain and Sea Power, 1815–53*, Oxford, 1963; A. Lambert, *Battleships in Transition: the creation of the steam battlefleet, 1815–60*, London, 1984; A. J. Marder: *The Anatomy of British Sea Power: a history of British naval policy in the pre-Dreadnought era, 1880–1905*, New York, 1940; *From the Dreadnought to Scapa Flow: the Royal Navy in the Fisher era*, 5 vols., London, 1961–78; and J. T. Sumida, *In Defence of Naval Supremacy, 1889–1914*, Boston and London, 1989.

New light is thrown on the history of the army in the years following Waterloo by M. Partridge in N. Gash, editor, *Wellington: studies in the military and political career of the first Duke of Wellington*, Manchester, 1990. I. F. W. Beckett and J. Gooch, editors, *Politicians and Defence: studies in the formulation of British defence policy 1845–1970*, Manchester, 1981, deal with aspects of military administration from 1847 to 1914. Edward M. Spiers, *The Late Victorian Army, 1868–1902*, Manchester 1992, highlights recruiting problems and the effects of the Boer War in a most comprehensive study. The years immediately before 1914 are examined by J. Gooch, *The Plans of War: the general staff and British military strategy, c. 1906–16*, London, 1974; David French, *British Economic and Strategic Planning, 1905–15*, London, 1982; E. M. Spiers, *Haldane: an Army reformer*, Edinburgh, 1980.

Extended bibliographies of British foreign policy can be found in Chamberlain and Bourne above, and the interaction of foreign and defence policy is discussed in many of the detailed works already mentioned. The following is a selection of the studies the present author found to be of particular interest. These often range more widely than their titles suggest. See especially M. Yapp, *Strategies of British India: Britain, Iran and Afghanistan, 1789–1850*, Oxford 1980; K. Bourne, *Britain and the Balance of Power in North America, 1815–1908*, London, 1967; E. Ingram, *The Beginning of the Great Game in Asia, 1818–34*, Oxford, 1979; A. Lambert, *The Crimean War: British grand strategy, 1853–56*, Manchester, 1990; R. Millman, *British Policy and the Coming of the Franco-Prussian War*, Oxford, 1965; R. Millman, *Britain and the Eastern Question, 1875–78*, Oxford, 1979; C. J. Lowe, *Salisbury and the Mediterranean, 1886–96*, London, 1965; R. L. Greaves, *Britain and the Defence of Persia, 1884–92*, London 1959; K. M. Wilson, *The Policy of Entente: the determinants of British foreign policy, 1904–14*, Cambridge, 1985; Z. S. Steiner, *Britain and the Origins of the First World War*, London, 1977.

Index